VOLUME 2 CONTENTS

W9-BWJ-377

***** This lesson consists only of activities from the Teacher's Guide.

Houghton Mifflin

Math Expressions

Volume 2

Developed by
The Children's Math Worlds
Research Project

PROJECT DIRECTOR AND AUTHOR

Dr. Karen C. Fuson

This material is based upon work supported by the
National Science Foundation
under Grant Numbers
ESI-9816320, REC-9806020, and RED-935373.

Any opinions, findings, and conclusions or recommendations expressed in this
material are those of the author and do not necessarily reflect the views of the
National Science Foundation.

HOUGHTON MIFFLIN   BOSTON

Teacher Reviewers

Kindergarten

Patti Sugiyama
Wilmette, Illinois

Barbara Wahle
Evanston, Illinois

Grade 1

Megan Rees
Chicago, Illinois

Sandra Budson
Newton, Massachusetts

Grade 2

Janet Pecci
Chicago, Illinois

Molly Dunn
Danvers, Massachusetts

Agnes Lesnick
Hillside, Illinois

Grade 3

Sandra Tucker
Chicago, Illinois

Jane Curran
Honesdale, Pennsylvania

Grade 4

Sara Stoneberg Llibre
Chicago, Illinois

Sheri Roedel
Chicago, Illinois

Grade 5

Todd Atler
Chicago, Illinois

Leah Barry
Norfolk, Massachusetts

Credits

Cover art: (stopwatch) © Photodisc/Getty Images. (cheetah) © John Daniels/Ardea London Ltd. (train) © Michael Dunning/Photographer's Choice/Getty Images.

Illustrative art: Dave Klug.
Technical art: Morgan-Cain & Associates

Printed in the U.S.A.

ISBN: 0-618-50993-3

1 2 3 4 5 6 7 8 9 KDL 11 10 09 08 07 06

Name   **Date**

▶ Shifts With Whole Numbers

Jordan earns $243 a week. The money is shown at the right. Answer the questions about how much he will earn over time.

Jordan's Weekly Earnings

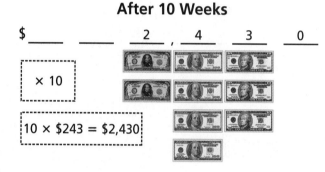

$\_\_\_\_ \_\_\_\_ \_\_\_\_ \quad 2 \quad 4 \quad 3$

×1

$1 \times \$243 = \$243$

1. After 10 weeks, how much will Jordan have earned?

_____

2. What happens to each $1-bill when it is multiplied by 10?

_____

After 10 Weeks

$\_\_\_\_ \_\_\_\_ \quad 2 , 4 \quad 3 \quad 0$

×10

$10 \times \$243 = \$2,430$

3. What happens to each other bill when it is multiplied by 10?

_____

4. When you multiply by 10, does each digit shift to the right or left?

_____

5. How many places does each digit shift?

_____

6. After 100 weeks, how much will Jordan have earned?

_____

7. What happens to each $1-bill when it is multiplied by 100?

_____

8. What happens to each digit when it is multiplied by 100?

_____

9. When you multiply by 100, does each digit shift to the right or left?

_____

10. How many places does each digit shift?

_____

After 100 Weeks

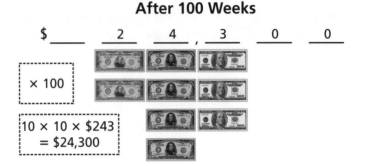

$ _____ 2 4 , 3 0 0

× 100

10 × 10 × $243 = $24,300

11. After 1,000 weeks, how much will Jordan have earned?

_____

12. What happens to each $1-bill when it is multiplied by 1,000?

_____

13. What happens to each digit when it is multiplied by 1,000?

_____

14. When you multiply by 1,000, does each digit shift to the right or left?

_____

15. How many places does each digit shift?

_____

After 1,000 Weeks

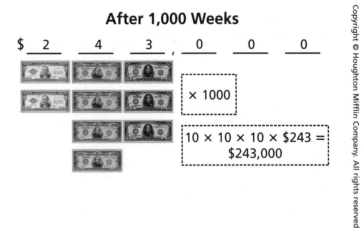

$ 2 4 3 , 0 0 0

× 1000

10 × 10 × 10 × $243 = $243,000

Name _____ **Date** _____

Class Activity

▶ See the Shift in Motion

Isabel earns $325 a week. Three students can show how the digits shift at the board when we multiply her earnings.

Complete each exercise.

16. Suppose Isabel works for 10 weeks. Find her earnings.

   ___ ___ ___ $ 3   2   5 | × 10 ⟩ $ ___ ___ 3 , 2 5 0

   $325 shifts ___ place(s) to the ___. It gets 10 times as great.

17. Suppose Isabel works for 100 weeks. Find her earnings.

   ___ ___ ___ $ 3   2   5 | × 100 ⟩ $ ___ 3 2 , 5 0 0

   $325 shifts ___ places to the ___. It gets 100 times as great.

18. Suppose Isabel works for 1,000 weeks. Find her earnings.

   ___ ___ ___ $ 3   2   5 | × 1,000 ⟩ $ 3 2 5 , 0 0 0

   $325 shifts _____ places to the ___. It gets 1,000 times as great.

Complete each exercise.

19. 567 × 10 = _____   20. 38 × 1,000 = _____

21. 912 × 100 = _____   22. 700 × 10 = _____

23. The Skyway Express train travels about 800 miles a day. How far does it travel in 10 days?

   _____

24. If there are 30 days in April, about how far will the train travel during the month of April?

   _____

Class Activity

Name _____ Date _____

► Shifts With Decimal Amounts

It costs $0.412 (41 and 2/10 cents) for a factory to make a Red Phantom marble. The money is shown here.

Cost of a Red Phantom Marble

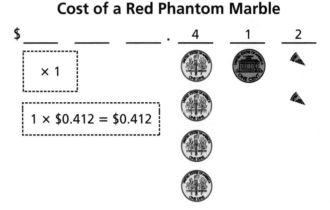

$ ____ ____ ____ . 4   1   2

× 1

1 × $0.412 = $0.412

Answer each question about the cost of making different numbers of Red Phantom marbles.

25. How much does it cost to make 10 Red Phantom Marbles?

_____

10 Red Phantom Marbles

$ ____ ____ 4 . 1   2 ____

× 10

10 × $0.412 = $4.12

26. What happens to each coin when it is multiplied by 10?

_____

27. What happens to each digit?

_____

28. When you multiply by 10, does each digit shift to the right or left?

_____

29. How many places does each digit shift?

_____

Shift Patterns in Multiplication

30. How much does it cost to make
    100 Red Phantom Marbles?

    _____

100 Red Phantom Marbles

$ ____ __4__ __1__ . __2__ __0__ ____

31. What happens to each coin
    when you multiply by 100?

    _____

× 100

32. What happens to each digit?

    _____

100 × $0.412 = $41.20

33. When you multiply by 100,
    does each digit shift to the
    right or left?

    _____

34. How many places does each digit shift?

    _____

35. How much does it cost to make
    1,000 Red Phantom Marbles?

    _____

1,000 Red Phantom Marbles

$ __4__ __1__ __2__ . __0__ __0__ ____

36. What happens to each coin
    when you multiply by 1,000?

    _____

× 1,000

37. What happens to each digit?

    _____

1,000 × $0.412 = $412.00

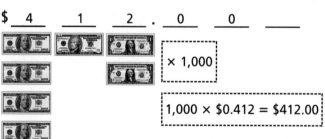

38. When you multiply by 1,000,
    does each digit shift to the
    right or left?

    _____

39. How many places does each digit shift?

    _____

Class Activity

▶ Patterns in Multiplying With Zeros

Discuss patterns you see across each row and down each column. Then state the Big Idea for multiplying numbers with zeros.

×	3	30	300	3,000
2	**a.** 2 × 3 = 6	**b.** 20 × 3 = 2 × 3 × 10 = 6 × 10 = 60	**c.** 2 × 300 = 2 × 3 × 100 = 6 × 100 = 600	**d.** 2 × 3,000 = 2 × 3 × 1,000 = 6 × 1,000 = 6,000
20	**e.** 20 × 3 = 2 × 10 × 3 = 6 × 10 = 60	**f.** 20 × 30 = 2 × 10 × 3 × 10 = 6 × 100 = 600	**g.** 20 × 300 = 2 × 10 × 3 × 100 = 6 × 1,000 = 6,000	**h.** 20 × 3,000 = 2 × 10 × 3 × 1,000 = 6 × 10,000 = 60,000
200	**i.** 200 × 3 = 2 × 100 × 3 = 6 x 100 = 600	**j.** 200 × 30 = 2 × 100 × 3 × 10 = 6 × 1,000 = 6,000	**k.** 200 × 300 = 2 × 100 × 3 × 100 = 6 × 10,000 = 60,000	**l.** 200 × 3,000 = 2 × 100 × 3 × 1,000 = 6 × 100,000 = 600,000
2,000	**m.** 2,000 × 3 = 2 × 1,000 × 3 = 6 × 1,000 = 6,000	**n.** 2,000 × 30 = 2 × 1,000 × 3 × 10 = 6 × 10,000 = 60,000	**o.** 2,000 × 300 = 2 × 1,000 × 3 × 100 = 6 × 100,000 = 600,000	**p.** 2,000 × 3,000 = 2 × 1,000 × 3 × 1,000 = 6 × 1,000,000 = 6,000,000

40. Big Idea: _____

Solve.

41.　　60
　　× 　3

42.　　60
　　× 30

43.　　600
　　× 　30

44.　　600
　　× 300

45.　6,000
　　× 　30

　　　　　　　　　　Shift Patterns in Multiplication

Dear Family,

Your child is familiar with multiplication and division problems from past years. Unit 4 of *Math Expressions* guides students as they deepen and extend their mastery of these operations. The main goal of this unit is to enhance skills in multiplying and dividing with whole numbers and decimal numbers. Some additional goals are:

• to solve real-world application problems,

• to use patterns as an aid in calculating,

• to use estimation to check the reasonableness of answers,

• to understand how to convert fractions to decimals, and

• to interpret remainders.

Your child will learn and practice techniques such as Rectangle Sections, Expanded Notation, and Shift Patterns to gain speed and accuracy in multiplication and division. Money examples will be used in multiplication and division with decimals.

Your child will learn to round and estimate, and then adjust the estimated number. Remainders will be interpreted in real-world contexts, and expressed as fractions or decimals. Students will divide by decimal numbers, and learn to distinguish between multiplication and division when there are decimal numbers.

Throughout unit 4, your child will solve real-world application problems that require multi-digit multiplication and division.

If you have any questions, please call or write to me.

Sincerely,
Your Child's Teacher

Estimada familia,

Su niño o niño ya se ha familiarizado con problemas de multiplicación y división en años pasados. La unidad 4 de *Math Expressions* guía a los estudiantes mientras profundizan y amplían su dominio de estas operaciones. El objetivo principal de la unidad es reforzar las destrezas de multiplicación y división de números enteros y decimales. Algunos objetivos adicionales son:

• resolver problemas con aplicaciones a la vida diaria,

• usar patrones de ayuda para hacer cálculos,

• usar la estimación para comprobar lo razonables que son las respuestas,

• comprender cómo se convierten las fracciones a decimales, e

• interpretar los residuos.

Su niño o niña aprenderá y practicará técnicas como secciones de rectángulos, notación desarrollada y patrones de valor relativo para poder hacer las multiplicaciones y divisiones con mayor rapidez y exactitud. En las multiplicaciones y divisiones con decimales, se usarán ejemplos de dinero.

Su niño o niña aprenderá a redondear y estimar, y luego a ajustar el número estimado. Los residuos se interpretarán dentro de contextos de la vida diaria y se expresarán como fracciones o decimales. Los estudiantes dividirán por números decimales y aprenderán a distinguir entre la multiplicación y la división con números decimales.

A lo largo de la unidad 4 su niño o niña resolverá problemas con aplicaciones a la vida diaria que requieren la multiplicación y división de números de varios dígitos.

Si tiene alguna duda o comentario, por favor comuníquese conmigo.

Atentamente,
El maestro o la maestra de su niño o niña

Shift Patterns in Multiplication

Class Activity

Name _____ **Date** _____

Vocabulary
Rectangle Sections
partial products

▶ Solve With Rectangle Sections

Think about finding the area of this rectangle (Area = length × width). It would be difficult to find 43 × 67 in one step. But if you broke the rectangle into smaller **Rectangle Sections**, then you could do it.

When you multiply larger numbers, you often need to break the problem into smaller parts. The products of these smaller parts are called **partial products**. After you find all the partial products, you can add them together.

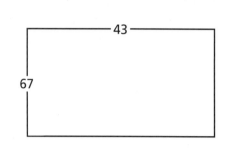

1. Explain how Rectangle Sections are used to solve the problem below.

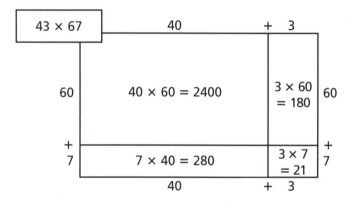

_____

_____

_____

2. Use Rectangle Sections to solve the multiplication problem below.

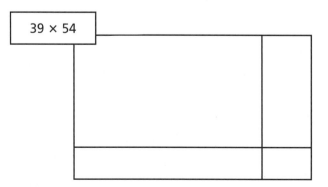

Class Activity

▶ Solve With Expanded Notation

Look at the **Expanded Notation** method of solving below.
Diagrams A and B both show the Expanded Notation method.
Diagram B only shows the results of the steps.

3. How is this method like the Rectangle Sections? How is it different?

_____

_____

43 × 67

A

```
43 = 40 + 3          ──────────►
× 67 = 60 + 7
    40 × 60 = 2400
     3 × 60 =  120
     7 × 40 =  280
     7 ×  3 =   21
              2,106
```

B

```
      43
    × 67
    2400
     180
     280
      21
   2,106
```

4. This rectangle shows the same problem. Can you relate the rectangle sections (a, b, c, d) to the 4 partial products shown in the Expanded Notation method above? Draw a line connecting each rectangle section to the partial product it shows.

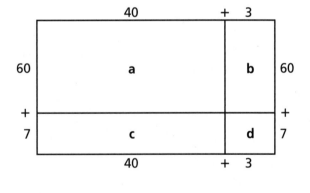

Solve. Use any method you like.

Show your work.

5. There are 32 cattle cars on today's train to Detroit. Each car holds 28 cows. How many cows are on the train?

_____

6. Maria jogs 21 miles every week. If there are 52 weeks in a year, how many miles does Maria jog in a year?

_____

Class Activity

Name _____   **Date** _____

Vocabulary

Rectangle Sections
partial products

▶ Solve With Rectangle Sections

Think about finding the area of this rectangle (Area = length × width). It would be difficult to find 43 × 67 in one step. But if you broke the rectangle into smaller **Rectangle Sections**, then you could do it.

When you multiply larger numbers, you often need to break the problem into smaller parts. The products of these smaller parts are called **partial products**. After you find all the partial products, you can add them together.

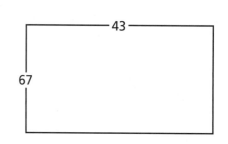

1. Explain how Rectangle Sections are used to solve the problem below.

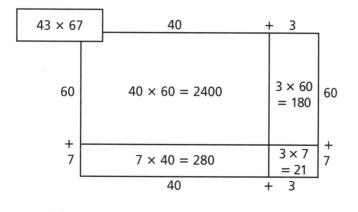

_____

_____

_____

2. Use Rectangle Sections to solve the multiplication problem below.

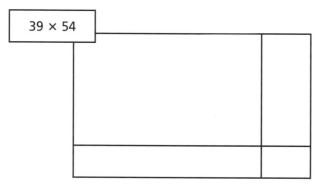

Vocabulary
Expanded Notation

▶ **Solve With Expanded Notation**

Look at the **Expanded Notation** method of solving below.
Diagrams A and B both show the Expanded Notation method.
Diagram B only shows the results of the steps.

3. How is this method like the Rectangle Sections? How is it
   different?

   _____

   _____

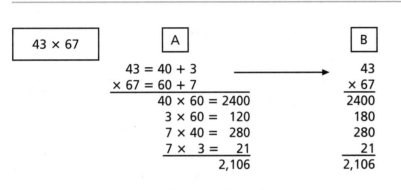

4. This rectangle shows the same problem.
   Can you relate the rectangle sections (a,
   b, c, d) to the 4 partial products shown in
   the Expanded Notation method above?
   Draw a line connecting each rectangle
   section to the partial product it shows.

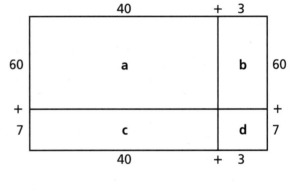

Solve. Use any method you like.

Show your work.

5. There are 32 cattle cars on today's train to Detroit. Each
   car holds 28 cows. How many cows are on the train?

   _____

6. Maria jogs 21 miles every week. If there are 52 weeks in
   a year, how many miles does Maria jog in a year?

   _____

The Area Model for Multiplication

Class Activity

Name _____ **Date** _____

Vocabulary

Rectangle Rows

► Methods for Two-Digit Multiplication

Look at the multiplication problem shown here. It is solved with another rectangle method called **Rectangle Rows**.

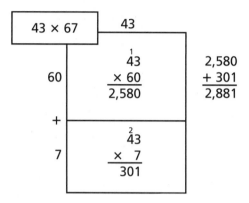

43 × 67	43

```
           1
          43          2,580
  60    × 60        + 301
        2,580         2,881
  +
           2
          43
   7    ×  7
          301
```

1. Explain the steps of the Rectangle Rows method.

_____

_____

_____

_____

2. How is the Rectangle Rows method different from the Rectangle Sections method you used yesterday?

_____

_____

_____

Use the Rectangle Rows method to solve each problem.

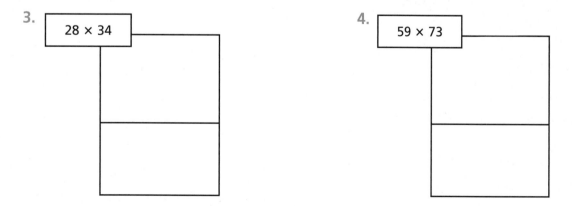

3.

28 × 34	

4.

59 × 73	

4–3 **Class Activity**

Name ____________________ Date ____________

Vocabulary
Short Cut

Here, 43 × 67 is solved with a method we call the **Short Cut**.

Step 1	Step 2	Step 3	Step 4	Step 5
			1	1
2	2	2	2	2
43	43	43	43	43
× 67	× 67	× 67	× 67	× 67
1	301	301	301	301
		0	2,580	2,580
				2,881

5. Explain the different steps of this method.

____

____

____

____

____

____

6. Why do we begin Step 3 by putting a zero in the ones place?

____

____

____

____

7. How is the Short Cut method like the Rectangle Rows method? How is it different?

____

____

____

____

____

____

Name _____   Date _____

▶ Discuss Multiplication Methods

Look at these 4 multiplication methods:

Rectangle Sections (page 00)   **Rectangle Rows (page 00)**
Expanded Notation (page 00)   **Short Cut (page 00)**
Use these questions for discussion.

8. Why are there more partial products in Rectangle Sections and Expanded Notation?

_____

_____

_____

_____

_____

9. How are the four partial products in Rectangle Sections and Expanded Notation related to the two partial products in Rectangle Rows and Short Cuts?

_____

_____

_____

10. The Short Cut method can be completed two ways. One way starts with the tens and the other way starts with the ones. Could we start with the ones for the other methods? Explain.

_____

_____

Solve.

11.   94
    × 36

12.   73
    × 45

13.   69
    × 82

14.   58
    × 70

Going Further

▶ Work Backward

Some problems are easiest to solve if you work backward.

Suppose you want to solve this problem: Julian has 5 times as many baseball cards as Carla. Carla has 8 times as many cards as Pete. Pete has 6 cards. How many cards does Julian have?

Answer these questions to solve the problem by working backward.

1. How many cards does Pete have?

   _____

2. Carla has 8 times as many cards as Pete. How many cards does Carla have?

   _____

3. Julian has 5 times as many cards as Carla. How many cards does Julian have?

   _____

4. Look back and check. Write the steps of your check.

   _____

   _____

Work backward to solve each problem.

5. Barbara spent half of her money at the mall. Then she spent half of what was left at the video store. She had $37 when she came home. How much money did Barbara have when she started at the mall?

6. Paul gave Brenda one third of his pretzels. Brenda shared her pretzels equally with Edwin. Edwin had 40 pretzels. How many pretzels did Paul have before he gave Brenda the pretzels?

7. A number is multiplied by 12 and then that result is doubled. The final result is 288. What is the number?

8. You multiply a number by 10 and then divide the result by 5. The final result is 90. Find the starting number.

Multiply Two-Digit Numbers

Class Activity

▶ Multiply Three-Digit Numbers

1. Below are the four multiplication methods your class has tried.
Circle the methods your group tried. Put a checkmark beside
the one that worked best. Which methods seem better for
problems with larger numbers? Why?

_____

_____

_____

_____

267 × 943	200	+	60	+	7	
900	180,000		8,000		600	900
+						+
40	54,000		2,400		180	40
+						+
3	6,300		280		21	3
	200	+	60	+	7	

```
  1 2 1  1
180,000
  8,000
    600

 54,000
  2,400
    180

  6,300
    280
     21
 ───────
251,781
```

```
943 = 900 + 40 + 3
× 267 = 200 + 60 + 7
─────────────────────
                 1 2 1  1
200 × 900 = 180,000
200 ×  40 =   8,000
200 ×   3 =     600

 60 × 900 =  54,000
 60 ×  40 =   2,400
 60 ×   3 =     180

  7 × 900 =   6,300
  7 ×  40 =     280
  7 ×   3 =      21
            ─────────
              251,781
```

	267
900	267 × 200 ───── 188,600
+	
40	267 × 60 ───── 56,580
+	
3	267 × 7 ───── 6,601

```
  1 2 1
188,600
 56,580
+ 6,601
────────
251,781
```

Multiply by Ones First

```
   2 1
   3 2
   943
×  267
   1 2 1
─────────
  6,601
 56,580
188,600
─────────
251,781
```

or

Multiply by Hundreds First

```
   3 2
   2 1
   943
×  267
   1 2 1
─────────
188,600
 56,580
  6,601
─────────
251,781
```

Class Activity

▶ Word Problems With Large Numbers

Two scientists went to Egypt to measure some of the ancient monuments there. Help them figure out the information they need to know.

Solve.

2. The Sphinx is a huge statue with the body of a lion and the head of a human. It was built thousands of years ago and still sits in the middle of the desert. The Sphinx is about 80 yards long. If there are 3 feet in a yard, how long is the Sphinx in feet?

   _____

3. The base of the Great Pyramid is a square about 150 feet on each side. How many square feet of ground does it cover?

   _____

4. Some of the blocks used to build the pyramids weigh up to 14 tons. If a ton is equal to 2,000 pounds, how much does one of these large blocks weigh in pounds?

   _____

5. If we include the end zones, a football field is 360 feet by 160 feet. What is the area of a football field in square feet?

   _____

6. The largest Egyptian pyramid covers an area as large as 10 football fields. What area is covered by the largest Egyptian pyramid?

   _____

7. The scientists stayed in Egypt for a year and traveled about 145 miles each day. If there are 365 days in a year, how far did they travel that year?

   _____

Multiply With Larger Numbers

▶ **Patterns With Fives**

1. Write an answer to the Puzzled Penguin.

> **The Puzzled Penguin**
>
> Dear Math Students:
>
> I know that when you multiply two numbers together, the product has the same number of zeros as the two factors. For example, 60 X 20 is 1200. There are two zeros in the factors (60 and 20) and two zeros in the product (1200).
>
> I am confused about one thing. I know that 50 X 2 is 100, and I am quite sure that 50 X 4 is 200. In these two problems, there is only one zero in the factors, but there are **two** zeros in the product. The pattern I learned does not seem to be true in these cases.
>
> Did I make a mistake somewhere?
>
> The Puzzled Penguin

_____

_____

_____

2. Find each product to complete the chart below. One factor in each problem contains a 5. Discuss the patterns you see for the number of zeros in each product. How does the number of zeros in the product relate to the number of zeros in the factors?

_____

_____

5 × 20	=	5 × 2 × 10	=	10 × 10	=
50 × 40	=	5 × 10 × 4 × 10	=	20 × 100	=
50 × 600	=	5 × 10 × 6 × 100	=	30 × 1,000	=
500 × 800	=	5 × 100 × 8 × 100	=	40 × 10,000	=

Name _____   Date _____

3. Find each product to complete the chart below. Again, one factor in each problem contains a 5. How does the number of zeros in the product relate to the number of zeros in the factors?

_____

_____

5 × 30	=	5 × 3 × 10	=	15 × 10	=
50 × 50	=	5 × 10 × 5 × 10	=	25 × 100	=
50 × 700	=	5 × 10 × 7 × 100	=	35 × 1,000	=
500 × 900	=	5 × 100 × 9 × 100	=	45 × 10,000	=

4. Explain why the product sometimes has an "extra" zero.

_____

_____

▶ Solve Fives-Pattern Problems

Tell how many zeros there will be. Then solve.

5.   80
   × 5
   _____

6.   70
   × 5
   _____

7.   90
   × 50
   _____

8.   60
   × 50
   _____

Solve.

9. Ernesto and his sister Dora are playing a computer game. Ernesto has earned 236 points so far. His sister has earned 50 times as many points. How many points has Dora earned?

_____

10. Mount Whitney is the tallest mountain in the lower 48 states of the United States. It is about 14,500 feet tall. Mount Everest is the tallest mountain in the world. It is twice as tall as Mount Whitney. About how tall is Mount Everest?

_____

Class Activity

▶ Computation Practice

Solve. Use scratch paper or work in your Math Journal.

1.	35	2.	74	3.	67	4.	18
	× 90		× 40		× 41		× 72

5.	82	6.	96	7.	153	8.	216
	× 76		× 43		× 79		× 74

9.	653	10.	584	11.	213	12.	406
	× 89		× 75		×479		×124

▶ Practice With Word Problems

Solve.

Show your work.

13. The planet Mercury has a diameter of 3,100 miles. Neptune's diameter is 10 times Mercury's diameter. What is Neptune's diameter?

_____

14. A movie theater has 16 rows of seats, with 36 seats in each row. What is the total number of seats in the theater?

_____

15. A large package of toothpicks contains 425 toothpicks. If Kerry buys 24 packages, how many toothpicks will she have?

_____

16. Paolo's car can travel 285 miles on each tank of gasoline. How many miles can the car travel on 20 tanks of gasoline?

_____

17. Farmer Ruben's rectangular wheat field is 789 meters by 854 meters. What is the area of this wheat field?

_____

Name _____   **Date** _____

Going Further

Vocabulary

estimate
overestimate

▶ Estimate Products

You can **estimate** to check if an answer is reasonable or to see when an exact answer is not needed. You estimate to find about how many or how much.

Carrie wants to estimate 411×87. She rounds each factor to its greatest place and then multiplies. 411×87 is about 36,000.

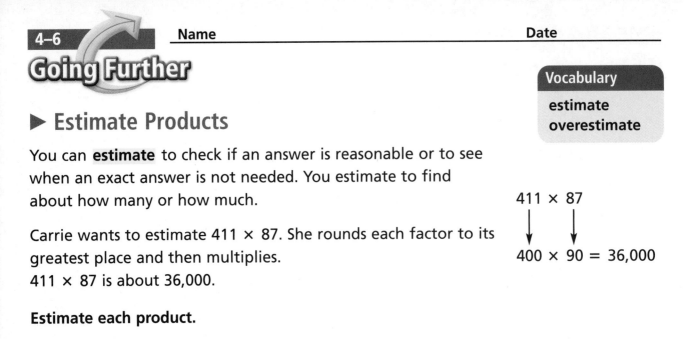

411×87

$400 \times 90 = 36,000$

Estimate each product.

1. 68×41 _____
2. 62×619 _____
3. 57×829 _____
4. 309×513 _____

Sometimes you need to **overestimate** to be sure you have enough.

Mr. Poy is planning a trip for 64 students. The cost will be $19 per student. To be sure he allows enough money in the budget, he overestimates. He rounds each factor up and then multiplies. By overestimating, he knows that $1,400 is more than he needs.

64×19

$70 \times 20 = 1,400$

Solve. Decide whether to estimate, overestimate, or find the exact answer.

5. There are 21 crates of oranges. Each crate weighs 195 pounds. About how many pounds of oranges are there?

6. Akule's family uses an average of 597 gallons of water per day. About how many gallons will they use in one month?

7. Ms. Long has 12,000 cans of juice. There are 543 students, and there are 18 school days in May. Is there enough for every student to get one can of juice each school day in May? Explain.

8. Erin is making programs for a play. Each program has 9 sheets of paper. Last year, 445 programs were used. Erin wants to overestimate to be sure she has enough paper. How many sheets of paper should she order?

Multiplication Practice

Name _____

Date _____

▶ Decimals in Money Situations

The Ruiz children had a yard sale. They sold some old toys. They made a table to show how many toys they sold and how much money they earned.

jump ropes	9 cents	3 × 9 cents = 27 cents	3 × $0.09 = $0.27
marbles	2 cents	4 × 2 cents = 8 cents	4 × $0.02 = $0.08
toy cars	12 cents	6 × 12 cents = 72 cents	6 × $0.12 = $0.72
puzzles	30 cents	5 × 30 cents = 150 cents	5 × $0.30 = $1.50

1. How did they know the number of decimal places in each product?

_____

_____

2. How much money did they earn?

_____

Mia saves the change from her lunch money each day. She gets $0.34 in change, and she has been saving it for 26 days. Mia used the steps below to find how much money she has saved so far.

$0.34 = $0.30 + $0.04
× 26 =   20 +   6

Step 1	Multiply by the number in the ones place (6).	6 × $0.04 = 6 × 4 cents = 24 cents = $0.24 6 × $0.30 = 6 × 30 cents = 180 cents = $1.80
Step 2	Multiply by the number in the tens place (2 tens = 20).	20 × $0.04 = 20 × 4 cents = 80 cents = $0.80 20 × $0.30 = 20 × 30 cents = 60 dimes = $6.00
Step 3	Add the partial products.	$8.84

3. How many decimal places are there in the decimal factor (0.34)? How many decimal places are there in the answer?

_____

Class Activity

Name _____

Date _____

A bead factory spends $0.346 to make each crystal bead. The steps below show how to find the total amount the factory spends to make 222 crystal beads.

$$\begin{array}{r} \$0.346 \\ \times \ \ 222 \end{array}$$

Step 1	Multiply by the number in the ones place.	2 × $0.346 = $0.692
Step 2	Multiply by the number in the tens place. (2 tens = 20; 0.692 shifts 1 place left.)	20 × $0.346 = $6.920
Step 3	Multiply by the number in the hundreds place. (2 hundreds = 200; 0.692 shifts 2 places left.)	200 × $0.346 = $69.200
Step 4	Add the partial products.	$76.812

4. How many decimal places are there in the decimal factor (0.346)? How many decimal places are there in the answer?

_____

5. Describe the relationship between the number of decimal places you have seen in a decimal product and the number of decimal places in its decimal factor.

_____

▶ Decimals in Other Situations

The owners of the Seven Seas Spice Company want to sell twice as much spice in the future as they do now. The table shows how much spice they sell in a week now and how much they want to sell in the future.

Cloves	0.3 ton	2 × 0.3 ton = 0.6 ton
Cinnamon	0.004 ton	2 × 0.004 ton = 0.008 ton
Ginger	0.007 ton	2 × 0.007 ton = 0.014 ton
Pepper	0.6 ton	2 × 0.6 ton = 1.2 tons

6. Look at the number of decimal places in each decimal factor and the number of decimal places in each product. What pattern do you see?

_____

7. Is this the same pattern you saw in problems 1–4?

_____

▶ Multiply With Decimals

Look at the patterns you have developed in exercises 1–7.

8. State the Big Idea for multiplying a whole number times a decimal number.

_____

_____

_____

_____

Find each product.
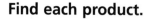

9. 0.8	10. 0.3	11. 0.005	12. 0.14	13. 0.43
× 6	× 40	× 9	× 32	× 64

Solve.

14. Jesse bought 3 aquariums. Each holds 8.75 gallons of water. How many gallons of water will they hold altogether?

_____

15. Jesse wants to buy 24 angelfish. Each angelfish costs $2.35. What will be the total cost of the angelfish?

_____

16. There are three goldfish in one of Jesse's aquariums. Gus is the smallest. He weighs only 0.98 ounce. Ella weighs 3 times as much as Gus. What is Ella's weight?

_____

17. Otto weighs 7 times as much as Gus. What is Otto's weight?

_____

Going Further

▶ Zero Patterns in Decimal Places

You have seen patterns in multiplying by multiples of 10. You have seen patterns in multiplying by decimals. You can use these two patterns together. The table below shows how you can multiply decimals by whole numbers, using:

• ones, tens, and hundreds
• tenths, hundredths, and thousandths

x	0.3	0.03	0.003
2	2 × 0.3 = 2 × 3 × 0.1 = 6 × 0.1 = 0.6	2 × 0.03 = 2 × 3 × 0.01 = 6 × 0.01 = 0.06	2 × 0.003 = 2 × 3 × 0.001 = 6 × 0.001 = 0.006
20	20 × 0.3 = 2 × 10 × 3 × 0.1 =60 × 0.1 = 6.0	20 × 0.03 = 2 × 10 × 3 × 0.01 = 60 × 0.01 = 0.60	20 × 0.003 = 2 × 10 × 3 × 0.001 = 60 × 0.001 = 0.060
200	200 × 0.3 = 2 × 100 × 3 × 0.1 = 600 × 0.1 = 60.0	200 × 0.03 = 2 × 100 × 3 × 0.01 = 600 × 0.01 = 6.00	200 × 0.003 = 2 × 100 × 3 × 0.001 = 600 × 0.001 = 0.600

Find each product using the method shown in the table above.

1. 4 × 0.2 = _____

2. 5 × 0.6 = _____

3. 40 × 0.07 = _____

4. 300 × 0.3 = _____

5. 200 × 0.08 = _____

Multiply Decimals by Whole Numbers

Name _____ **Date** _____

Class Activity

▶ Shifts With Decimals

Leon earns $213 a month. The money is shown here. He will save some of it every month.

Leon's Earnings

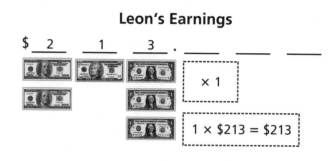

$ __2__ __1__ __3__ . ____ ____ ____

× 1

1 × $213 = $213

Answer the questions about the different savings plans.

1. If he saves 0.1 of his earnings, how much will he save each month?

   _____

Save 0.1 Each Month

$____ __2__ __1__ . __3__ __0__ ____

× 0.1

0.1 × $213 = $21.30

2. What happens to each bill?

   _____

3. What happens to each digit?

   _____

4. When you multiply by 0.1, does each digit shift to the right or left?

   _____

5. How many places does each digit shift?

   _____

6. If he saves 0.01 of his earnings, how much will he save each month?

_____

7. What happens to each bill?

_____

8. What happens to each digit?

_____

9. When you multiply by 0.01, does each digit shift to the right or left?

_____

10. How many places does each digit shift?

_____

Save 0.01 Each Month

$ ____ ____ 2 . 1 3 ____

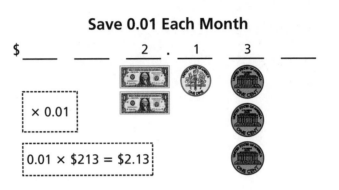

× 0.01

0.01 × $213 = $2.13

11. If he saves 0.001 of his earnings, how much will he save each month?

_____

12. What happens to each bill?

_____

13. What happens to each digit?

_____

14. When you multiply by 0.001, does each digit shift to the right or left?

_____

15. How many places does each digit shift?

_____

Save 0.001 Each Month

$ ____ ____ 0 . 2 1 3

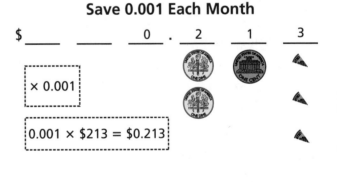

× 0.001

0.001 × $213 = $0.213

Class Activity

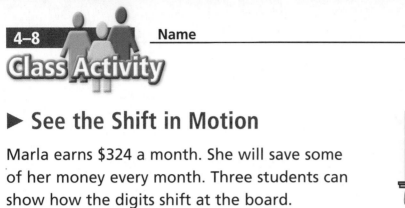

▶ See the Shift in Motion

Marla earns $324 a month. She will save some of her money every month. Three students can show how the digits shift at the board.

Complete each exercise.

16. Suppose Marla saves 0.1 of $324 every month.

$ 3 ___ 2 ___ 4 · ___ ___ ___ ⟩× 0.1⟩ $ ___ 3 ___ 2 · 4 ___ 0 ___

   $324 shifts _____ place(s) to the _____. It becomes _____ as much.

17. Suppose Marla saves 0.01 of $324 every month.

$ 3 ___ 2 ___ 4 · ___ ___ ___ ⟩× 0.01⟩ $ ___ ___ 3 · 2 ___ 4 ___

   $324 shifts _____ place(s) to the _____. It becomes _____ as much.

18. Suppose Marla saves 0.001 of $324 every month.

$ 3 ___ 2 ___ 4 · ___ ___ ___ ⟩× 0.001⟩ $ ___ ___ 0 · 3 ___ 2 ___ 4

   $324 shifts _____ place(s) to the _____. It becomes _____ as much.

Name _____   **Date** _____

▶ Shifts When Both Factors Are Decimals

Multiply by one tenth. Think about what it means to take one tenth of another part.

19. 0.1 × 0.4 = _____ Think: What is one tenth of one tenth? Then, what is one tenth of four tenths?

20. 0.1 × 0.04 = _____ Think: What is one tenth of one hundredth? Then, what is one tenth of four hundredths?

21. How many places did the 4 shift each time you multiplied? _____ In which direction? _____

22. Look at your answers. What pattern do you see in the number of decimal places in the products? How is it related to the number of places in the two factors?

_____

_____

_____

Multiply by one hundredth. Think about what it means to take one hundredth of another part.

23. 0.01 × 0.4 = _____ Think: What is one hundredth of one tenth? Then, what is one hundredth of four tenths?

24. 0.01 × 0.04 = _____ Think: What is one hundredth of one hundredth? Then, what is one hundredth of four hundredths?

25. How many places did the 4 shift each time you multiplied? _____ In which direction? _____

26. Look at your answers. What pattern do you see in the number of decimal places in the products? How is it related to the number of places in the two factors?

_____

_____

_____

Multiply by Decimals

27. How could you express the Big Idea about the number of decimal places in the product when you multiply a decimal number by another decimal number? Is it the same as the Big Idea for multiplying a decimal number by a whole number?

_____

_____

_____

_____

28. To multiply by 2 tenths or 2 hundredths, you could think of 2 tenths as 2 × 0.1 and 2 hundredths as 2 × 0.01.

0.2 × 0.4 = (2 × _____) × 0.4 = 2 × (0.1 × 0.4) = 2 × 0.04 = _____

0.02 × 0.4 = (2 × _____) × 0.4 = 2 × (0.01 × 0.4) = 2 × 0.004 = _____

Is your Big Idea about the number of decimal places in the product still true? _____

Use the shift pattern to solve each multiplication. Check to see if the Big Idea works.

29. 0.2 × 0.4 = _____

30. 0.2 × 0.04 = _____

31. 0.2 × 0.004 = _____

32. 0.02 × 0.4 = _____

33. 0.02 × 0.04 = _____

34. 0.02 × 0.004 = _____

35. 0.002 × 0.4 = _____

36. 2 × 0.4 = _____

Using the Big Idea you just discovered, solve each multiplication.

37. 0.3 × 0.4 = _____

38. 0.3 × 0.04 = _____

39. 0.3 × 0.004 = _____

40. 0.03 × 0.4 = _____

41. 0.03 × 0.04 = _____

42. 0.03 × 0.004 = _____

43. 0.003 × 0.4 = _____

44. 3 × 0.4 = _____

Solve.

Show your work.

45. Benjamin bought 6.2 pounds of rice. Each pound cost $0.90. How much did he spend on rice?

_____

46. Sabrina walks 0.85 mile to school. Kirk walks only 0.3 as far as Sabrina. How far does Kirk walk to school?

_____

47. Isabel wrote 4 letters to her pen pals. For each letter she bought a stamp. Each stamp cost $0.60. How much did she spend on stamps?

_____

48. Maura rode her bike 5 laps around the block. Each lap is 0.45 mile. How many miles did she ride?

_____

49. Kim bought 2 pounds of baked turkey that cost $5.98 per pound. What was the total cost?

_____

Name _____ **Date** _____

▶ Compare Whole Number and Decimal Multipliers

Complete each sentence.

Whole Number Multipliers

1. When you multiply by 10, the number gets _____ times as big. The places shift _____ place(s) to the _____.

3. When you multiply by 100, the number gets _____ times as big. The places shift _____ place(s) to the _____.

5. When you multiply by 1,000, the number gets _____ times as big. The places shift _____ place(s) to the _____.

Decimal Number Multipliers

2. When you multiply by 0.1, the number gets _____ as big. The places shift _____ place(s) to the _____.

4. When you multiply by 0.01, the number gets _____ as big. The places shift _____ place(s) to the _____.

6. When you multiply by 0.001, the number gets _____ as big. The places shift _____ place(s) to the _____.

7. How is multiplying by 10 or 100 or 1,000 like multiplying by 0.1 or 0.01 or 0.001? How is it different?

_____

_____

_____

_____

For each exercise, discuss the shift. Then find each product.

8. $\begin{array}{r} 3.6 \\ \times\ 10 \\ \hline \end{array}$

9. $\begin{array}{r} 3.6 \\ \times\ 0.1 \\ \hline \end{array}$

10. $\begin{array}{r} 3.6 \\ \times\ 100 \\ \hline \end{array}$

11. $\begin{array}{r} 3.6 \\ \times\ 0.01 \\ \hline \end{array}$

12. $\begin{array}{r} 3.6 \\ \times\ 1,000 \\ \hline \end{array}$

13. $\begin{array}{r} 3.6 \\ \times\ 0.001 \\ \hline \end{array}$

14. $\begin{array}{r} 3.6 \\ \times\ 1 \\ \hline \end{array}$

15. $\begin{array}{r} 3.6 \\ \times\ 1.0 \\ \hline \end{array}$

▶ Extend and Apply the Big Idea

Zeros at the end of a decimal number do not change the value of the number. Remember this as you explore the Big Idea about the number of decimal places in a product.

These exercises all have an "extra" zero in the product because of the 5-pattern. Complete each multiplication.

16. 0.5 × 2 = _____

17. 0.08 × 0.5 = _____

18. 0.06 × 0.05 = _____

19. 0.4 × 0.5 = _____

20. Does the Big Idea about the product having the same number of decimal places as the two factors still work? _____

These problems are all the same, but are expressed in different ways. Multiply.

21. 3 × 3 = _____

22. 3.0 × 3 = _____

23. 3.0 × 3.0 = _____

24. 3.00 × 3.00 = _____

25. Does the Big Idea about the product having the same number of decimal places as the two factors still work? Do your answers all mean the same thing? _____

Solve.

Show your work.

26. Ada and her family are canoeing in the wilderness. They carry the canoe along trails between lakes. Their map gives each trail distance in rods. They know that a rod is equal to 5.5 yards. Find each trail distance in yards.

Black Bear Trail; 8 rods _____

Wild Flower Trail; 9.3 rods _____

Dark Cloud Trail; 24.1 rods _____

27. The world's largest diamond is the Star of Africa, which is 530.2 carats. A carat is about 0.2 gram. What is the weight of the Star of Africa in grams?

Class Activity

▶ Review of Rounding

Round each number.

1. Round 42 to the nearest ten. Which ten is closer to 42?

    _____

    50 ⌉

    42

    40 ⌋

2. Round 762 to the nearest hundred. Which hundred is closer to 762?

    _____

    800 ⌉

    762

    700 ⌋

3. Round 0.86 to the nearest tenth. Which tenth is closer to 0.86?

    _____

    0.9 ⌉

    0.86

    0.8 ⌋

4. Round 0.263 to the nearest hundredth. Which hundredth is closer to 0.263?

    _____

    0.27 ⌉

    0.263

    0.26 ⌋

Round to the nearest ten.

5. 46 _____   6. 71 _____   7. 85 _____   8. 928 _____

Round to the nearest hundred.

9. 231 _____   10. 459 _____   11. 893 _____   12. 350 _____

Round to the nearest tenth.

13. 0.73 _____   14. 0.91 _____   15. 0.15 _____   16. 0.483 _____

Round to the nearest hundredth.

17. 0.532 _____   18. 0.609 _____   19. 0.789 _____   20. 0.165 _____

Name _____

Date _____

▶ Explore Estimation in Multiplication

For each exercise, round the factors and multiply mentally to find the estimated answer. After finding all the estimated answers, go back and find each exact answer.

Estimated Answer	**Exact Answer**
21. 24 × 39 ≈ _____	24 × 39 = _____
22. 151 × 32 ≈ _____	151 × 32 = _____
23. 0.74 × 0.21 ≈ _____	0.74 × 0.21 = _____
24. 12.3 × 3.7 ≈ _____	12.3 × 3.7 = _____

25. Is there more than one way to round these numbers? Why are some exact answers closer to the estimated answer than others?

_____

_____

_____

▶ Use Estimation to Check Answers

26. Tanya did these multiplications on her calculator.

24.5 × 4 = 98   0.56 × 30 = 1.68   15.2 × 2.03 = 30.856

0.09 × 143 = 12.87   0.74 × 12.02 = 88.948   9.03 × 6.9 = 623.07

How can she use estimation to see if each answer makes sense? Which answers are clearly wrong?

_____

_____

_____

_____

▶ Ordinary Estimations and Safe Estimations

The Puzzled Penguin

Dear Math Students:

Yesterday I went to the store to buy 8 bottles of juice for a party. Each bottle cost $2.48, so I rounded to the nearest dollar, which is $2.00. My estimate for the total cost was 8 × $2.00 = $16.00. I had $18.00 in my pocket, so I thought everything was fine. When I went to the cashier to pay, I found out that I didn't have enough money. I was very embarrassed.

Is there something wrong with my math? Maybe estimation isn't very helpful when you're buying things.

The Puzzled Penguin

27. Respond to the Puzzled Penguin in your Math Journal.

Show your work.

For each problem below, decide whether you need to make a safe estimate or an ordinary estimate. Estimate the answer, and then find the exact answer.

28. Michelle and Stacy walked 9.95 miles every day for 14 days. How far did they walk altogether?

Safe estimate or ordinary estimate? _____

Estimate: _____   Exact answer: _____

29. Mrs. Reno is planning to buy 3 bicycles for her children. Each bicycle costs $144.78, including the tax. How much will Mrs. Reno need to buy all 3 bicycles?

Safe estimate or ordinary estimate? _____

Estimate: _____   Exact answer: _____

30. Each bag of soil in the Green Thumb Garden Center weighs 6.89 kilograms. There are 21 bags. What is the total weight of the bags?

Safe estimate or ordinary estimate? _____

Estimate: _____   Exact answer: _____

31. **On the Back** Explain your answer for problem 30. Which estimation did you choose? Why?

Name _____ Date _____

▶ Practice With Decimals

Suppose you know that 234 × 48 = 11,232. Use this to find each product.

1. 23.4 × 4.8 = _____   2. 0.234 × 4.8 = _____

3. 0.234 × 0.48 = _____   4. 0.48 × 2.34 = _____

5. 48 × 23.4 = _____   6. 4.8 × 2.34 = _____

7. 23.4 × 0.048 = _____   8. 2.34 × 0.048 = _____

9. 234 × 4.8 = _____   10. 48 × 0.234 = _____

Find each product. You may need scratch paper.

11.	12.	13.	14.
46	75	97	64
× 0.9	× 0.8	× 0.04	× 0.05

15.	16.	17.	18.
0.346	597	4.59	0.924
× 127	× 0.284	× 57.3	× 0.865

Round to the nearest tenth.

19. 0.68 _____   20. 0.93 _____   21. 0.841 _____   22. 0.092 _____

Round to the nearest hundredth.

23. 0.492 _____   24. 0.218 _____   25. 0.907 _____   26. 0.569 _____

▶ Solve Word Problems

Solve.

Show your work.

27. Marcus sails his boat 94.5 miles every day. If he sails for 25 days, how far will he travel in all?

_____

28. The distance around a circle (the circumference) is about 3.14 times the diameter. If a circular table has a diameter of 36 inches, what is the circumference?

_____

29. Nina is reading about red kangaroos. She found out that a male red kangaroo usually weighs about 66 kilograms, and a female red kangaroo usually weighs about 26.5 kilograms. One kilogram is about 2.2 pounds. What is the weight of a male red kangaroo in pounds?

_____

30. What is the weight of a female red kangaroo in pounds?

_____

31. A printer has 395 ink colors and 254 styles of letters (fonts). How many different combinations are possible?

_____

32. Jodie wants to buy a ticket for every basketball game this season. Tickets cost $16.50 each, and there are 15 games this season. How much will Jodie spend on tickets?

_____

Multiplication Practice

Name _____ **Date** _____

Going Further

▶ Use Calculation, Estimation, or Mental Math

There are different ways that you can solve problems depending upon the type of answer that you need.

- If the problem asks for an exact answer then you need to do the calculation.

USE CALCULATION

The cost of a movie ticket is $6.25. If 7 friends go to the movies, how much money will they need?

7 × $6.25 = $43.75

- If a question uses words such as *about*, *approximately*, *almost*, *nearly*, or *enough*, then you can estimate your answer.

USE ESTIMATION

Hector earns $8.05 per hour. Last week he worked 19.5 hours. About how much did he earn?

19.5 × $8.05 ≈ 20 × $8 = $160
Hector earned about $160.

- For some problems, you can use mental math.

USE MENTAL MATH

Angela is training for a race. Last week she ran 400 meters 15 times. How many meters did she run altogether?

15 × 400 = 15 × 4 × 100 =
60 × 100 = 6,000 meters

For each question, write whether to use calculation, estimation, or mental math. Then solve.

1. The Math Club is selling packs of paper for $1.95. The first week they sold 125 packs. The next week they sold 376 packs and the third week they sold 408 packs. About how much money did they collect in all?

   _____

2. The Math Club ordered 2,000 packs of paper. Each pack contains 150 sheets of paper. How many sheets is this in all?

   _____

   _____

➡ 3. **On the Back** Write and solve three multiplication word problems. Solve at least one by estimating.

Multiplication Practice **275**

Name _____ **Date** _____

Multiplication Practice

Name _____ **Date** _____

Class Activity

▶ Compare Division Methods

An airplane travels the same distance every day. It travels 3,822 miles in a week. Compare these methods of dividing that can be used to find how many miles the airplane travels each day.

Rectangle Sections

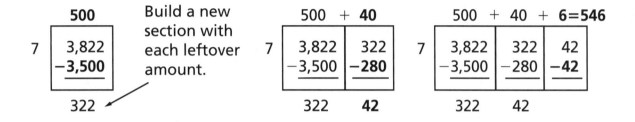

Expanded Notation

$$
\begin{array}{r}
500 \\
7\overline{)3,822} \\
-3,500 \\
\hline
322
\end{array}
$$

Show the zeroes in the place values.

$$
\begin{array}{r}
40 \\
500 \\
7\overline{)3,822} \\
-3,500 \\
\hline
322 \\
-280 \\
\hline
42
\end{array}
$$

$$
\begin{array}{r}
6 \\
40 \;\Big)\,546 \\
500 \\
7\overline{)3,822} \\
-3,500 \\
\hline
322 \\
-280 \\
\hline
42 \\
-42
\end{array}
$$

Digit-By-Digit

$$
\begin{array}{r}
5 \\
7\overline{)3,822} \\
-3,5 \\
\hline
32
\end{array}
$$

Put in only one digit at a time.

$$
\begin{array}{r}
54 \\
7\overline{)3,822} \\
-3,5 \\
\hline
32 \\
-28 \\
\hline
42
\end{array}
$$

$$
\begin{array}{r}
546 \\
7\overline{)3,822} \\
-3,5 \\
\hline
32 \\
-28 \\
\hline
42 \\
-42
\end{array}
$$

Name _____ **Date** _____

Class Activity

Vocabulary

remainder

▶ Division Problems

Solve.

1. A farmer has 2,106 cows and 9 barns. If the farmer divides the cows into equal groups, how many cows will he put in each barn?

_____

2. A sidewalk covers 3,372 square feet. If the sidewalk is 4 feet wide, what is its length?

_____

3. Olivia has $8. Her mother has $4,784. How many times as much money does Olivia's mother have as Olivia?

_____

4. A potter can make 2,513 different kinds of pots and bowls by combining different shapes and colors. If he knows how to make 7 different shapes, how many colors does the potter have?

_____

▶ Work With Remainders

This problem might seem unfinished. The leftover number at the bottom is called the **remainder**. We can write the answer like this: 567 R 2

```
       567
   8)4,538
   – 40
      53
    – 48
      58
    – 56
       2
```

5. Could there be a remainder of 9 for the problem above? Why or why not?

_____

_____

_____

6. What is the largest possible remainder when dividing by 8?

_____

Complete each division and give the remainder.

7. 6)5,380

8. 7)6,747

9. 5)4,914

Divide Whole Numbers by One Digit

Going Further

Name _____ **Date** _____

Vocabulary
mean
measure of central tendency

▶ Find the Mean

The **mean** is one way to describe a set of data. The mean, sometimes called the average, is a **measure of central tendency**.

To find the mean of a data set, follow these steps:
- Step 1: Add all of the numbers in the data set.
- Step 2: Divide the total by the number of numbers in the data set.

Example Find the mean of this data set: 40, 162, 100, 38.
- Step 1: 40 + 162 + 100 + 38 = 340
- Step 2: 340 ÷ 4 = 85
  The mean is 85.

Find the mean for each set of data.

Show your work.

1. 24, 27, 25, 24 _____

2. 13, 17, 14, 18, 15, 14, 14 _____

3. 1, 1, 4, 2, 1, 3, 1, 4, 2, 1 _____

4. 350, 400, 450, 100, 500 _____

Solve.

5. Jan's cousins are 144 cm, 150 cm, 131 cm, 160 cm, and 150 cm tall. What is the mean height of Jan's cousins?

_____

6. Mia's math test scores were 96, 80, 100, and 100. What was Mia's average math test score?

_____

7. There are 1,010 students at Ridge School. At Valley School, there are 851 students. At Park School, there are 860 students. What is the mean number of students for the three schools?

_____

8. **On the Back** Write and solve two problems that involve finding the mean.

Name _____ **Date** _____

► Division With Decimal Amounts

Three friends set up a lemonade stand and made $20.25. They will share the money equally. Study the steps below to see how much money each person should get.

When the $20 is split 3 ways, each person gets $6. There is $2 left.	We change the $2 to 20 dimes and add the other 2 dimes. There are 22 dimes.	When we split 22 dimes 3 ways, each person gets 7 dimes. There is 1 dime left.	We change the dime to 10 cents and add the other 5 cents. Now we split 15 cents 3 ways.
$$\begin{array}{r} 6 \\ 3\overline{)20.25} \\ -\,18 \\ \hline 2 \end{array}$$	$$\begin{array}{r} 6. \\ 3\overline{)20.25} \\ -\,18 \\ \hline 2.2 \end{array}$$	$$\begin{array}{r} 6.7 \\ 3\overline{)20.25} \\ -\,18 \\ \hline 2.2 \\ -\,2.1 \\ \hline .1 \end{array}$$	$$\begin{array}{r} 6.75 \\ 3\overline{)20.25} \\ -\,18 \\ \hline 2.2 \\ -\,2.1 \\ \hline .15 \\ -\,.15 \end{array}$$

Solve each decimal division exercise.

1. $8\overline{)47.68}$

2. $9\overline{)58.68}$

3. $6\overline{)316.2}$

Solve.

Show your work.

4. Imelda has 8.169 meters of rope. She wants to cut it into 3 equal pieces to make jump ropes for her 3 friends. How long will each piece of rope be?

_____

5. Tonio has 7.47 pounds of rabbit food. He will divide it equally among his 9 rabbits. How much food will each rabbit get?

_____

6. Discuss how dividing a decimal number is like dividing a whole number.

_____

Name _____   Date _____

Use multiplication to help you solve these problems.

7. 32 ÷ 8 = _____

   8 × _____ = 32

   8)‾32‾

8. 3.2 ÷ 8 = _____

   8 × _____ = 3.2

   8)‾3.2‾

9. 0.32 ÷ 8 = _____

   8 × _____ = 0.32

   8)‾0.32‾

10. 0.032 ÷ 8 = _____

   8 × _____ = 0.032

   8)‾0.032‾

Solve using mental math.

11. 6.3 ÷ 9 = _____

12. 0.15 ÷ 3 = _____

13. 4.8 ÷ 6 = _____

14. 0.021 ÷ 7 = _____

▶ Annex Zeros in the Dividend

Jun must run 6.65 miles every day for practice. She knows that if she runs half of that distance and back again she will have run enough miles. How far should Jun run before she turns around to run back?

```
    3.325
 2)6.650  ←—— She adds a zero to the
  −6              end of the decimal
 ‾‾‾‾            number.
  0.6
  .6
 ‾‾‾‾        This allows her to
   .05      finish solving the
   .04      problem.
 ‾‾‾‾
   .010 ◂
   .010
```

Solve each exercise.

15. 6)‾54.750‾

16. 5)‾141.20‾

17. 8)‾310.00‾

Divide Decimal Numbers by One Digit

Name _____   **Date** _____

▶ Write Fractions as Decimals

Fractions and decimals are both ways to show parts of a whole.

1. Divide 100 pennies into 4 equal parts.   2. Divide 100 pennies into 8 equal parts.

3. Write one fourth of a dollar as a decimal number: _____

4. Write one eighth of a dollar as a decimal number: _____

Use long division to write each fraction as a decimal.

5. $\frac{1}{4}$ $4\overline{)1.00}$ 6. $\frac{2}{4}$ $4\overline{)2.00}$ 7. $\frac{3}{4}$ $4\overline{)3.00}$ 8. $\frac{1}{8}$ $8\overline{)1.000}$

9. $\frac{2}{8}$ $8\overline{)2.000}$ 10. $\frac{3}{8}$ $8\overline{)3.000}$ 11. $\frac{4}{8}$ $8\overline{)4.000}$ 12. $\frac{5}{8}$ $8\overline{)5.000}$

13. $\frac{6}{8}$ $8\overline{)6.000}$ 14. $\frac{7}{8}$ $8\overline{)7.000}$

Use these number lines to discuss questions 15 and 16.

```
0.00           0.25           0.50           0.75           1.00
 |--------------|--------------|--------------|--------------|
 0              1              2              3              4
 ─              ─              ─              ─              ─
 4              4              4              4              4
```

```
0.000   0.125   0.250   0.375   0.500   0.625   0.750   0.875   1.000
 |-------|-------|-------|-------|-------|-------|-------|-------|
 0       1       2       3       4       5       6       7       8
 ─       ─       ─       ─       ─       ─       ─       ─       ─
 8       8       8       8       8       8       8       8       8
```

15. What patterns do you see?

_____

16. Which decimal numbers are equal in value?

_____

17. Divide 100 pennies into 5 equal parts.

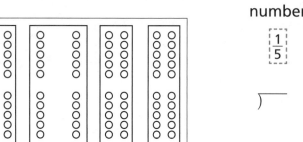

18. Use long division to find the decimal numbers for fifths.

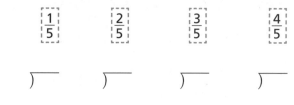

$\frac{1}{5}$ $\frac{2}{5}$ $\frac{3}{5}$ $\frac{4}{5}$

19. Make a number line showing the decimal numbers and fractions for fifths.

0.0   1.0

$\frac{0}{5}$ $\frac{5}{5}$

20. Divide 100 pennies into 3 equal parts.   21. Divide 100 pennies into 6 equal parts.

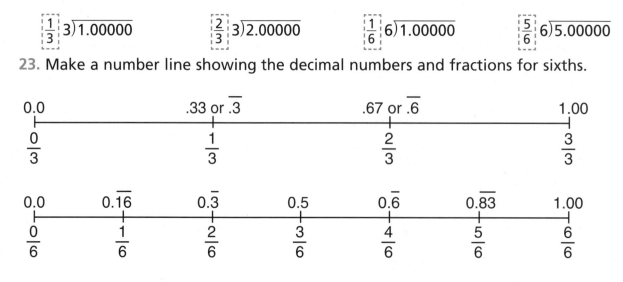

22. Use long division to find the decimal numbers for thirds and sixths.

$\frac{1}{3}$ $3\overline{)1.00000}$ $\frac{2}{3}$ $3\overline{)2.00000}$ $\frac{1}{6}$ $6\overline{)1.00000}$ $\frac{5}{6}$ $6\overline{)5.00000}$

23. Make a number line showing the decimal numbers and fractions for sixths.

0.0   .33 or .$\overline{3}$ .67 or .$\overline{6}$ 1.00

$\frac{0}{3}$ $\frac{1}{3}$ $\frac{2}{3}$ $\frac{3}{3}$

0.0   0.1$\overline{6}$ 0.$\overline{3}$ 0.5   0.$\overline{6}$ 0.8$\overline{3}$ 1.00

$\frac{0}{6}$ $\frac{1}{6}$ $\frac{2}{6}$ $\frac{3}{6}$ $\frac{4}{6}$ $\frac{5}{6}$ $\frac{6}{6}$

Name _____ **Date** _____

▶ Word Problems

In baseball and softball, a batting average describes how well a player hits. (It is not a mean!) To find a player's batting average, write a fraction showing the number of hits over the number of at bats, and then write that fraction as a decimal with three places.

Solve.

Show your work.

24. In the first four games of the season, Lauryn got 3 hits in 9 at bats. What was her batting average?

_____

25. Felicia is on a softball team. In her first 8 at bats, she got 5 hits. What was her batting average?

_____

26. On Saturday, Allie played baseball with her family. She had 3 at bats and got 2 hits. What was her batting average?

_____

27. Carl's baseball team had a picnic. The coach bought $3\frac{1}{2}$ pounds of potato salad for the picnic, paying $2.25 per pound. How much did the potato salad cost?

_____

28. At the team picnic, the players raced on an obstacle course that the coach planned. The first part of the race was on a trail $\frac{3}{8}$ mile long. The second part was on a park road 0.4 mile long. What was the total length of the race?

_____

Name _____ **Date** _____

Going Further

▶ Problems Involving Means

Remember how to find the mean of a data set:

- Add all of the numbers in the data set.

- Divide the total by the number of items in the data set.

When data items are fractions, it is often helpful to first write them as decimals.

Example Tyra is training for a race. She ran these distances last week:

$3\frac{1}{2}$ miles, $3\frac{1}{4}$ miles, $4\frac{1}{8}$ miles, 4 miles, and $3\frac{2}{5}$ miles. To find the mean, she wrote all the fractions in decimal form and then calculated.

Tyra's mean training distance was 3.655 miles.

$$
\begin{array}{r}
3.5 \\
3.25 \\
4.125 \\
4 \\
+\ 3.4 \\
\hline
18.275
\end{array}
$$

$$
\begin{array}{r}
3.655 \\
5\overline{)18.275}
\end{array}
$$

Solve.

Show your work.

1. Tyra drinks a lot of water on the day of a race. At the last race she drank $1\frac{1}{2}$ cups, $1\frac{7}{8}$ cups, and 3 cups. What was the mean amount of water that Tyra drank?

_____

2. Sam works at a deli counter. His boss asked him to find the mean weight of the next four customer orders. The orders were: $1\frac{1}{4}$ pounds of ham, $1\frac{1}{2}$ pounds of cheese, 2 pounds of turkey, and $2\frac{1}{4}$ pounds of roast beef. What was the mean weight?

_____

3. Tony and his friends sold snacks at the school play to raise money for the Drama Club. They collected $12.50 for muffins, $3.75 for apples, $5.60 for cranberry juice, $12.50 for soft pretzels, $16.00 for frozen yogurt, and $1.40 for carrot sticks. What was the mean amount collected?

_____

Express Fractions as Decimals

Class Activity

Name _____   Date _____

▶ # Experiment With Two-Digit Divisors

Vocabulary

estimate
Digit by Digit
Expanded Notation
Rectangle Sections

When we divide by a two-digit number, we build the unknown factor place by place just as we did before. But this time we must **estimate** each number in the answer.

There are 2,048 sheep being sent on a train. Each railroad car holds 32 sheep.

To find how many railroad cars are needed for the sheep, divide 2,048 by 32.

Here are three methods to divide 2,048 by 32. Discuss the steps in each method.

DIVISION PROBLEMS WITH STEPS AS SHOWN

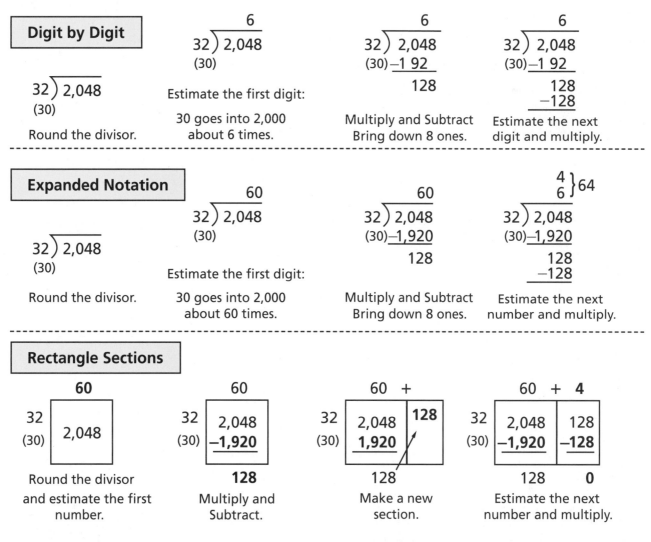

Class Activity

Name _____ Date _____

Look at exercises 1–3. Would you round the divisor up or down to estimate the first number? Complete each exercise, using any method you choose.

1. 79)4,032

2. 21)1,533

3. 18)1,061

▶ Does Estimation Always Work?

Complete exercise 4 together as a class. Does the rounding give you a correct estimate of the first digit? Does it give you a correct estimate of the next digit? Discuss what you can do to finish the problem.

4. 54)3,509

Complete and discuss each exercise below.

5. 74)3,651

6. 42)3,231

7. 23)1,892

Explore Dividing by Two-Digit Whole Numbers

Name _____

Date _____

Class Activity

► Underestimating

Here are two ways to divide 5185 ÷ 85. Discuss each method and answer the questions with your class.

How do we know that the first estimated number is not right? What number should we try next? Solve the problem using that number.

How do we know that the first estimated number is not right this time? Do we need to erase, or could we just finish solving the problem? Try it.

1. When we estimate with a number that is too big (overestimate), we have to erase and change the number. When we estimate with a number that is too small (underestimate), do we always have to erase? Explain your answer.

_____

_____

_____

_____

_____

Solve each division. You may need to adjust one or both of the estimated numbers.

2. $56\overline{)4,032}$ 3. $77\overline{)4,791}$ 4. $18\overline{)798}$

Class Activity

Name _____ Date _____

Think about what kind of divisor is most likely to lead to an estimated number that is wrong. Test your idea by doing the first step of each problem below.

5. 41)2,583
   246
   _____
   12

6. 34)1,525
   136
   _____
   16

7. 29)928
   87
   _____

8. 16)1,461
   144
   _____
   2

9. What kind of divisor is most likely to lead to an estimated number that is wrong?

_____

_____

▶ Mixed Practice With Adjusted Estimates

Solve.

10. Hector picked 1,375 oranges in his fruit orchard. He will pack them in crates to take to market. Each crate holds 24 oranges.

    How many crates will Hector fill? _____

    How many oranges will be left over? _____

11. The skateboards at the Speed Demon Shop sell for $76 each. This week the shop owner sold $5,396 worth of skateboards. How many skateboards were sold?

    _____

12. Ashley's dog Tuffy eats 21 ounces of dog food for each meal. Ashley has 1,620 ounces of food in the house.

    How many meals will Tuffy have before Ashley needs to buy more food? _____

    How many ounces of food will be left after the last meal? _____

Too Large, Too Small, or Just Right?

▶ Decide What to Do With the Remainder

When you divide to solve a problem, you need to decide what to do with the remainder to answer the question.

Think about each of these ways to use a remainder. Solve each problem. Show your work.

Sometimes you ignore the remainder.

1. The gift-wrapping department of a store has a roll of ribbon 1,780 inches long. It takes 1 yard of ribbon (36 inches) to wrap each gift.

   How many gifts can be wrapped?

   _____

   Why do you ignore the remainder?

   _____

   _____

   _____

Sometimes you round up to the next whole number.

2. There are 247 people traveling to the basketball tournament by bus this year. Each bus holds 52 people.

   How many buses will be needed?

   _____

   Why do you round up?

   _____

   _____

   _____

   _____

Sometimes you use the remainder to form a fraction.

3. The 28 students in Mrs. Colby's class will share 98 slices of pizza equally at the class picnic.

   How many slices will each student get?

   _____

   Look at the division shown here. Explain how to get the fraction after you find the remainder.

   _____

   _____

   _____

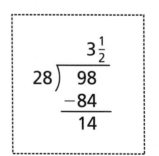

$$28\overline{)98} \quad 3\tfrac{1}{2}$$
$$\underline{-84}$$
$$14$$

4–17

Name _____ **Date** _____

Sometimes you use a decimal number instead of the remainder.

Suppose 16 friends earned $348 at a car wash, and they want to divide the money equally. To find how much each person will get, one of the friends divided as shown here. Each friend will get $21.75.

```
        21.75
16) 348.00
   −32
    28
    16
   120
   112
    80
    80
```

4. A rectangular garden has an area of 882 square meters. The long side of the garden is 35 meters long. How long is the short side?

_____

Sometimes the remainder is the answer to the problem.

5. A bagel shop has 138 bagels to be packed into boxes of 12 to be sold. The extra bagels are for the workers.

   How many bagels will the workers get? _____
   Why is the remainder the answer?

_____

_____

_____

▶ Practice Solving Problems Involving Remainders

Solve.

Show your work.

6. At the Cactus Flower Cafe, all the tips are divided equally among the waiters. Last night the 16 waiters took in $1,108. How much did each waiter get in tips?

_____

7. A gardener needs to move 2,150 pounds of dirt. He can carry 98 pounds in his wheelbarrow. How many trips will he need to make with the wheelbarrow?

_____

Interpret Remainders

Class Activity

Name _____   **Date** _____

Solve.

Show your work.

8. Mia must work 133 hours during the month of May. There are 21 working days in May this year. How many hours per day will Mia work if she works the same number of hours each day?

_____

9. Colored markers cost 78 cents each. Pablo has $8.63 in his pocket. How many colored markers can Pablo buy?

_____

10. A meat packer has 180 kilograms of ground meat. He will divide it equally into 50 packages. How much will each package weigh?

_____

11. In volleyball there are 12 players on the court. If 75 people all want to play volleyball at a gym that has more than enough courts, how many of them must sit out at one time?

_____

12. At the Fourth of July celebration, 1,408 ounces of lemonade will be shared equally by 88 people. How many ounces of lemonade will each person get?

_____

13. Armando needs quarters to ride the bus each day. He took $14.87 to the bank and asked to have it changed into quarters. How many quarters did he get?

_____

14. **On the Back** Write and solve two division word problems. Each problem should use a different way to interpret the remainder.

Interpret Remainders

Class Activity

▶ Use Money to See Shift Patterns

Jordan earns $243 a week. The money is shown here.

Jordan's Earnings in Dollars

$ _____ _____ _____ 2 4 3

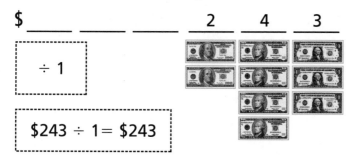

÷ 1

$243 ÷ 1 = $243

Answer each question about how much he earns in coins.

1. How many dimes ($0.10) does he earn?

   _____

2. What happens to each dollar?

   _____

3. What happens to the number showing Jordan's earnings?

   _____

4. When you divide by 0.1, does each digit shift right or left?

   _____

5. How many places does each digit shift?

   _____

Jordan's Earnings in Dimes

$ _____ _____ 2 , 4 3 0

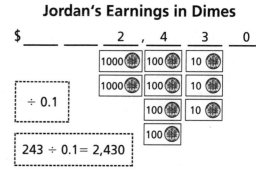

÷ 0.1

243 ÷ 0.1 = 2,430

6. How many pennies ($0.01) does he earn?

_____

7. What happens to each dollar?

_____

8. What happens to the number showing Jordan's earnings?

_____

9. When you divide by 0.01, does each digit shift right or left?

_____

10. How many places does each digit shift?

_____

Jordan's Earnings in Pennies

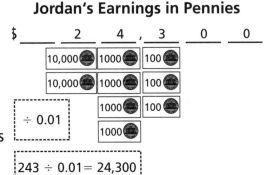

11. How many tenths of a cent ($0.001) does he earn?

_____

12. What happens to each dollar?

_____

13. What happens to the number showing Jordan's earnings?

_____

14. When you divide by 0.001, does each digit shift right or left?

_____

15. How many places does each digit shift?

_____

Jordan's Earnings in Tenths of a Cent

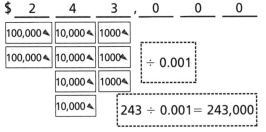

Divide Whole Numbers by Decimal Numbers

Class Activity

Name

Date

▶ Relate Decimal Division to Multiplication

Solve.

Show your work.

16. Mrs. Moreno made 1 liter of grape jelly. She will pour it into jars that each hold 0.1 of a liter. How many jars will she need?

Think: How many tenths are there in 1 whole? _____

Complete the equation: 1 ÷ 0.1 = _____

This is the same as 1 × _____

17. Mr. Moreno made 2 liters of spaghetti sauce. He will also pour it into jars that each hold 0.1 of a liter. How many jars will he need?

Think: How many tenths are there in 1 whole? _____

In 2 wholes? _____

Complete the equation: 2 ÷ 0.1 = _____

This is the same as 2 × _____

18. The Morenos made a kiloliter of fruit punch for a large party. They will pour it into punch bowls that each hold 0.01 kiloliter. How many bowls will they need?

Think: How many hundredths are there in 1 whole? _____

Complete the equation: 1 ÷ 0.01 = _____

This is the same as 1 × _____

19. Why do we get a larger number when we divide by a decimal number that is less than one?

_____

_____

_____

The Puzzled Penguin

Dear Math Students:

One of my friends says that dividing a number by one tenth (0.1) is the same as multiplying the number by 10. He also says that dividing by one hundredth (0.01) is the same as multiplying by 100. He thinks this is also true for one thousandth, one millionth, and so on.

Is he right? I don't see how this can be true. Usually multiplication gives us a larger number, and division gives us a smaller number. So this would be very strange. Can you explain it?

The Puzzled Penguin

20. _____

_____

_____

_____

▶ Change Decimal Divisors to Whole Numbers

It is easier to divide when the divisor is a whole number. We can change the divisor to a whole number by using the strategy below.

Discuss each step used to find 6 ÷ 0.2.

Understand the Division Problem

Step 1: We know that 6 ÷ 0.2 can be written as a fraction: ⟶ $6 \div 0.2 = \frac{6}{0.2}$

Step 2: We can make an equivalent fraction with a whole number divisor by multiplying the top and bottom by 10. Now we can divide 60 by 2. ⟶ $\frac{6 \times 10}{0.2 \times 10} = \frac{60}{2} = 2\overline{)60}$

21. Why will the answer to 60 ÷ 2 be the same as the answer to 6 ÷ 0.2?

_____

_____

_____

Divide Whole Numbers by Decimal Numbers

Solve with long division.

Step 1: We can show this multiplication by 10 in long division. First, put a decimal point in the product: ⟶ $0.2\overline{)6.}$

Step 2: Then we multiply both numbers by 10, moving the decimal points one place to the right and writing zeros if necessary: ⟶ $0.2_\wedge\overline{)6.0_\wedge}$

Step 3: We don't have to draw arrows. A little mark called a caret (^) shows where we put the "new" decimal points. Now we divide 60 by 2, just as we did with equivalent fractions. ⟶ $0.2_\wedge\overline{)6.0_\wedge}\ ^{30}$

22. Why can we simply move both decimal points and get the same answer?

_____

_____

Answer each question to describe how to find 6 ÷ 0.02 and 6 ÷ 0.002.

23. Suppose you want to find 6 ÷ 0.02.

By what number can you multiply 0.02 to get a whole number?

_____

Describe how to move the decimal points to solve 6 ÷ 0.02 by long division.

_____

24. Suppose you want to find 6 ÷ 0.002.

Describe how to move the decimal points to solve 6 ÷ 0.002.

_____

25. $0.5\overline{)45}$ 26. $0.07\overline{)56}$ 27. $0.8\overline{)496}$ 28. $0.65\overline{)910}$

➡ 29. **On The Back** Describe how to use long division to find 40 ÷ 0.005.

▶ Use Money to See Shift Patterns

It costs $0.312 (31 cents and $\frac{2}{10}$ cent) to make
one Cat's Eye Marble. The money is shown here.

Cost of a Cat's Eye Marble

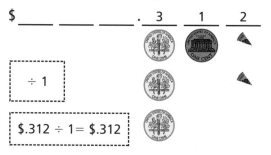

Answer each question about the different coins.

1. How many dimes ($0.10) does it cost to make
   one Cat's Eye Marble?

   _____

2. What happens to the number that shows
   the cost?

   _____

3. When you divide by 0.1 does each digit shift to
   the right or left?

   _____

4. How many places does each digit shift?

   _____

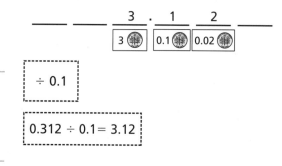

5. How many cents ($0.01) does it cost to make one Cat's Eye Marble?

_____

6. What happens to the number that shows the cost?

_____

7. When you divide by 0.01, does each digit shift to the right or left?

_____

8. How many places does each digit shift?

_____

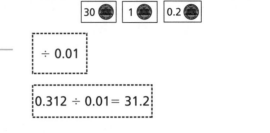

```
_____  3   1 . 2  _____ _____
      [30]  [1] [0.2]
```

```
÷ 0.01
```

```
0.312 ÷ 0.01 = 31.2
```

9. How many tenths of a cent ($0.001) does it cost to make one Cat's Eye Marble?

_____

```
 3   1   2 . _____ _____ _____
[300][10] [2]
```

```
÷ 0.001
```

10. What happens to the number that shows the cost?

_____

```
0.312 ÷ 0.001 = 312
```

11. When you divide by 0.001, does each digit shift to the right or left?

_____

12. How many places does each digit shift?

_____

13. Compare the shift pattern in this lesson with the shift pattern in Lesson 18. Is the shift pattern for dividing by decimals the same when the product is a decimal number as when the product is a whole number? Why or why not?

_____

_____

_____

Divide With Two Decimal Numbers

Name _____   **Date** _____

▶ Change Decimal Divisors to Whole Numbers

What happens when there are two decimal numbers? We can use the same strategy as before, changing the divisor to a whole number.

Discuss each step used to find 0.06 ÷ 0.2.

14. Understand the Division Problem

Step 1: We know we can write 0.06 ÷ 0.2 as a fraction: ⟶ $0.06 \div 0.2 = \dfrac{0.06}{0.2}$

Step 2: We can make an equivalent fraction with a whole number divisor by multiplying the top and bottom by 10. Now we divide 0.6 by 2. Why does 0.06 ÷ 0.2 give the same answer as 0.6 ÷ 2?   ⟶ $\dfrac{0.06 \times 10}{0.2 \times 10} = \dfrac{0.6}{2} = 2\overline{)0.6}$

_____

_____

15. Solve With Long Division

Step 1: We can show this multiplication by 10 in a long division problem. First, we set up the problem: ⟶ $0.2\overline{)\,.06}$

⟶ $0.2\,\overbrace{)}\,.0\,6$

Step 2: Then we multiply both numbers by 10, moving the decimal points one place to the right and adding zeros if necessary: ⟶ $0.2_\wedge\overline{)\,.0_\wedge6}^{\,.3}$

Step 3: We don't have to draw arrows. The caret (^) shows where each "new" decimal point belongs. Now we divide 0.6 by 2, just as we did with equivalent fractions.

Why can we simply move both decimal points and get the same answer?

_____

_____

Class Activity

16. How would you solve 0.06 ÷ 0.02 with long division? What number do you need to multiply by to make 0.02 a whole number?

_____

_____

_____

_____

17. How would you solve 0.06 ÷ 0.002 with long division? What number do you need to multiply to make 0.002 a whole number?

_____

_____

_____

_____

Solve each division problem. Show your work.

18. $0.9\overline{)7.2}$

19. $0.04\overline{)0.364}$

20. $0.6\overline{)0.372}$

21. $0.14\overline{)7.28}$

22. A sand and gravel company has 12.6 tons of gravel to haul today. Each truck can carry 0.9 ton of gravel. How many trucks will be needed?

_____

23. Mountain climbers are climbing a trail that is 3.15 miles long. They can climb about 0.45 mile a day. How many days will it take them to reach the top?

_____

Divide With Two Decimal Numbers

Going Further

▶ Divisibility Rules for 2, 5, and 10

Vocabulary

divisible
even
odd

A number is **divisible** by another number if the remainder is zero when the first number is divided by the second number.

45 is divisible by 5 because the remainder is zero.

$$5\overline{)45} = 9$$

36 is not divisible by 5 because the remainder is not zero.

$$5\overline{)36} = 7\ R1$$

Here are rules you can use to test for divisibility without dividing.

Rule	Example	Example
A number is divisible by 2 if the ones digit is 0, 2, 4, 6, or 8.	136 is divisible by 2.	283 is not divisible by 2.
A number is divisible by 5 if the ones digit is 0 or 5.	1,760 is divisible by 5.	506 is not divisible by 5.
A number is divisible by 10 if the ones digit is 0.	790 is divisible by 10.	809 is not divisible by 10.

Complete the table. Use a check mark to show divisibility.

		24	65	110	108	137	215
1.	divisible by 2						
2.	divisible by 5						
3.	divisible by 10						

Even numbers are divisible by 2. **Odd** numbers are not divisible by 2.

Answer each question.

4. Write 5 numbers between 50 and 100 that are divisible by 5.

5. If a number is divisible by 10, what other numbers is it divisible by? Why?

6. **On The Back** Challenge: Write numbers that are divisible by 3. Find a pattern and write a rule. Test your rule.

Divide With Two Decimal Numbers

▶ Place-Value Concepts in Division

The Puzzled Penguin

Dear Math Students:

Today I am going to the store with my friend to buy some greeting cards that cost 75 cents each. I have $19.50 to spend. I want to know how many greeting cards I can buy. I solved the problem as shown below, but my friend said it was wrong. He said that if you move the decimal points two places to the right, then both numbers will get bigger and so your answer will be too big. Is he right? Why or why not?

$$0.75\overline{)19.50} = 0.\underset{\smile}{75}.\overline{)19.50.} = 75\overline{)1,950} = 75\overline{)1,950}^{\,26}$$

The Puzzled Penguin

---

1. Write a response to the Puzzled Penguin.

   _____

   _____

   _____

   _____

Suppose you know that 1,715 ÷ 35 = 49. Use this to solve each problem.

2. $35\overline{)17.15}$

3. $35\overline{)171.5}$

4. $0.35\overline{)0.1715}$

5. $35\overline{)17,150}$

6. $3.5\overline{)1,715}$

7. $0.35\overline{)1,715}$

8. $3.5\overline{)17.15}$

9. $0.35\overline{)0.1715}$

Class Activity

Name _____   **Date** _____

▶ Mixed Division Practice

Solve.

Show your work.

10. The Clark family is having a big lawn party. They have 196 chairs, and they want to put 8 chairs at each table. How many chairs will be left over?

_____

11. Liam needs to buy 640 eggs for a soccer breakfast. If eggs come in cartons of 18, how many cartons should he buy?

_____

12. Jacob made $507 this year delivering newspapers. How much money did he make each month?

_____

13. Ms. Uhura is making 12 skating costumes. She has 21 m of ribbon. How much ribbon can she use on each costume?

_____

14. A class trip will cost $358.40. There are 28 students in the class. How much will the trip cost per student?

_____

Division Practice

Class Activity

Solve.

Show your work.

15. The Ramsey family collects and sells maple syrup. Last month they collected 57.8 liters of syrup. They will pour it into bottles that hold 0.85 of a liter. How many bottles will the Ramseys fill?

_____

16. Kyle spent $22.94 on postage stamps today. Each stamp cost 37 cents ($0.37). How many stamps did Kyle buy?

_____

Solve.

17. $0.6\overline{)54}$

18. $0.08\overline{)72}$

19. $0.5\overline{)0.45}$

20. $0.04\overline{)28}$

21. $9\overline{)65}$

22. $0.07\overline{)0.49}$

23. $8\overline{)76}$

24. $0.05\overline{)34.5}$

25. $7\overline{)395}$

26. $0.6\overline{)141}$

27. $33\overline{)3,028}$

28. $0.045\overline{)41.85}$

29. **On The Back** Write and solve a division problem that uses a whole number and a decimal number.

Division Practice

► Decimal Multiplication or Decimal Division?

**For each problem, decide whether you need to multiply or divide.
Then solve.**

Show your work.

1. A certain turtle can walk 0.2 mile in one hour. How far
   can the turtle walk in 12 hours? How far can it walk in
   0.5 hour?

   _____

   _____

2. Gus runs 3.6 miles during running practice. He takes a sip
   of water for every 0.9 mile that he runs. How many sips
   does Gus take during his running practice?

   _____

   _____

3. Every year about 135 of the cows on Dixie's Dairy Farm
   have calves. This year only 0.6 as many cows had calves.
   How many cows had calves this year?

   _____

   _____

4. A box of oatmeal holds 1.2 pounds. Each bowl of
   oatmeal holds about 0.08 pound. How many bowls of
   oatmeal can you get from a box?

   _____

   _____

5. A rectangular patio has an area of 131.52 square meters.
   The width of the patio is 9.6 meters. What is its length?

   _____

   _____

▶ Results of Operations With Whole Numbers and Decimal Numbers

In the equations below, *a* and *b* are whole numbers larger than 1, and *d* is a digit so that 0.*d* is a decimal number smaller than 1. Answer each question.

6. If $b \times a = c$, is *c* larger or smaller than *a*? Why?

_____

_____

_____

7. If $0.d \times a = c$, is *c* larger or smaller than *a*? Why?

_____

_____

_____

8. If $a \div b = c$, is *c* larger or smaller than *a*? Why?

_____

_____

_____

9. If $a \div 0.d = c$, is *c* larger or smaller than *a*? Why?

_____

_____

_____

Answer each question without trying to find the value.

10. Which is larger, 42×356 or $356 \div 42$? How do you know?

_____

_____

_____

11. Which is larger, 0.65 × 561 or 561 ÷ 0.65? How do you know?

_____

_____

_____

12. Which is larger, 832 ÷ 67 or 832 ÷ 0.67? How do you know?

_____

_____

_____

13. Which is larger, 738 × 66 or 738 × 0.66? How do you know?

_____

_____

_____

_____

▶ **Make Predictions**

Solve.   *Show your work.*

14. Farmer Ortigoza has 124.6 acres of land. Farmer Ruben has 0.8 times as much land.

   Does Farmer Ruben have more or less than
   124.6 acres? _____

   How many acres does Farmer Ruben have? _____

15. Mee Young has 48 meters of crepe paper. She will cut it into strips that are each 0.6 meter long.

   Will Mee Young get more or fewer than
   48 strips? _____

   How many strips will Mee Young get? _____

Name _____   **Date** _____

Solve.

Show your work.

16. Roberto can lift 115 pounds. His friend Vance can lift 0.9 of that amount.

Can Vance lift more or less than 115 pounds? _____

How many pounds can Vance lift? _____

17. The Daisy Cafe served 18 liters of hot chocolate today. Each serving was in a cup that held 0.2 liter.

Did the cafe serve more or fewer than 18 cups of hot chocolate? _____

How many cups did the cafe serve? _____

▶ Mixed Practice

Solve.

18. $0.5 \times 3 =$ _____   **19.** $0.007 \times 6 =$ _____   **20.** $0.4 \times 0.8 =$ _____

21. $6\overline{)5.1}$ **22.** $4\overline{)22.8}$ **23.** $27\overline{)8.91}$ **24.** $34\overline{)1.564}$

25. $\begin{array}{r} 28 \\ \times\ 0.63 \\ \hline \end{array}$ **26.** $\begin{array}{r} 0.35 \\ \times\ \ 94 \\ \hline \end{array}$ **27.** $\begin{array}{r} 78.6 \\ \times\ \ 49 \\ \hline \end{array}$ **28.** $\begin{array}{r} 215 \\ \times\ 37 \\ \hline \end{array}$

29. $0.8\overline{)7.52}$ **30.** $0.03\overline{)0.285}$ **31.** $0.42\overline{)15.12}$ **32.** $1.9\overline{)1.634}$

Distinguish Between Multiplication and Division

33.   0.37
    × 0.09

34.   0.75
    × 0.14

35.   51.3
    × 6.2

36.   4.29
    × 0.27

37. 0.4)0.156

38. 0.13)689

39. 0.57)55.86

40. 0.96)460.8

▶ Mixed Real-World Applications

Solve.

Show your work.

41. The Fox Theater has 19 rows of seats with 26 seats in each row. There are 498 people standing in line to see a movie.

   How many people will get in? _____

   How many people will have to wait until the next movie? _____

42. Polly bought 12 beach balls for her beach party. She spent $23.64. How much did each beach ball cost?

   _____

43. All of the 245 fifth graders at Breezy Point School are going on a trip to the aquarium. Each van can carry 16 students.

   How many vans will be needed for the trip? _____

44. Today Aaliyah ran 4.5 miles per hour for three fourths (0.75) of an hour.

   How far did Aaliyah run today? _____

45. **On the Back** Write and solve two word problems involving decimals. One should require multiplication and one should require division.

Distinguish Between Multiplication and Division

Solve.

1. $\begin{array}{r} 100 \\ \times\ \ 35 \\ \hline \end{array}$

2. $\begin{array}{r} 4.8 \\ \times\ 0.01 \\ \hline \end{array}$

3. $0.1\overline{)4.5}$

4. $10\overline{)71.6}$

Solve. Use any method.

5. $\begin{array}{r} 73 \\ \times\ 81 \\ \hline \end{array}$

6. $\begin{array}{r} 349 \\ \times\ 28 \\ \hline \end{array}$

7. $\begin{array}{r} 64 \\ \times\ 57 \\ \hline \end{array}$

8. $\begin{array}{r} 472 \\ \times\ 370 \\ \hline \end{array}$

Solve.

9. $\begin{array}{r} 0.018 \\ \times\ \ \ \ 92 \\ \hline \end{array}$

10. $0.004 \times 0.8 =$ _____

11. **Circle the two multiplications that have the same product.**

    6×0.3 0.06×0.03 0.06×0.3 0.6×0.003 0.06×3

12. **Round the factors and multiply mentally to find the estimated answer. After finding the estimated answer, go back and find the exact answer.**

    Estimated Answer $0.53 \times 0.68 \approx$ _____

    Exact Answer $0.53 \times 0.68 =$ _____

Name _____   Date _____

13. Round the divisor up or down to estimate the first number. Complete using any method you choose.

$32\overline{)6,571}$

Divide.

14. $4\overline{)6,408}$ **15.** $0.7\overline{)567}$ **16.** $0.12\overline{)3.612}$

17. Circle the division that does not have the same answer as the others.

$72 \div 9$ $7.2 \div 0.9$ $0.72 \div 0.9$ $0.72 \div 0.09$ $0.072 \div 0.009$

For each problem, decide whether you need to multiply or divide. Then solve.

Show your work.

18. A large bag of pretzels contains 23.9 ounces. Five children want to share the pretzels equally. How many ounces of pretzels should each child get?

_____

19. Almonds cost $3.68 per pound. Hannah bought $11.04 worth of almonds. How many pounds of almonds did she buy?

_____

20. Extended Response Explain how to divide 1,105 by 17 using estimation to determine the first digit of the quotient.

_____

_____

_____

Vocabulary

rotation
reflection

▶ Discuss Rotations

You can rotate, or turn, a figure clockwise or counterclockwise about a point. The **rotation**, or movement of the figure, is measured in degrees (°). Each triangle below shows the result of a 90° counterclockwise rotation about point A, when point A is

inside the triangle.   on the triangle.   outside the triangle.

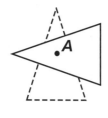
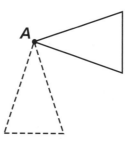
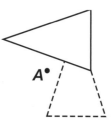

1. Cut out the figures on page 323. Work with a partner to show clockwise and counterclockwise rotations of 90°, 180°, and 270°.

2. Look at two consecutive figures in the pattern below. How many degrees has the figure been rotated? _____

3. Draw the fifteenth figure in the pattern. _____

▶ Discuss Reflections

You can reflect, or flip, a figure across a line. The line is called the line of **reflection**.

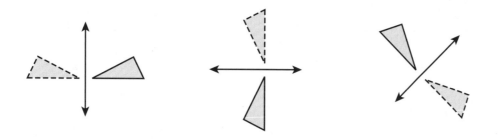

4. Using the figures you cut out and working on a grid, show a reflection across a line for each figure.

▶ Grid Paper

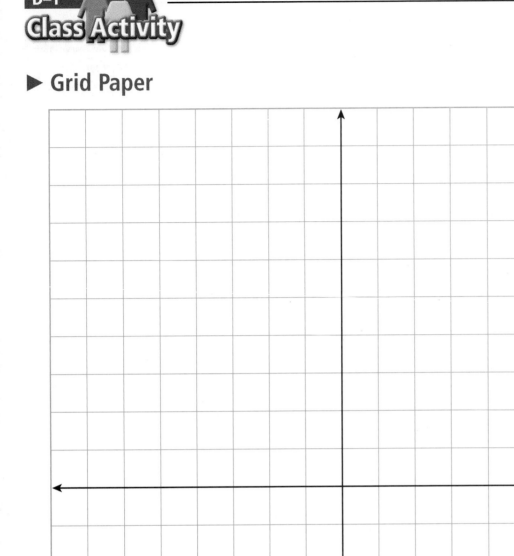

Explore Transformations

Name _____ **Date** _____

Vocabulary

translation
transformation

▶ Discuss Translations

A **translation** is a slide. When a figure is translated, each of its points moves the same distance in the same direction. These squares have been translated along the lines.

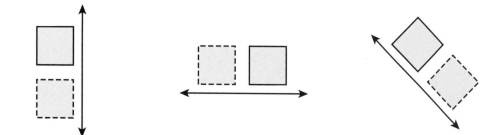

5. Use the figures you cut out on page 323 and, on a grid, show a translation along a horizontal line for each figure.

▶ Draw Transformations

Draw each transformation.

6. a reflection across the line

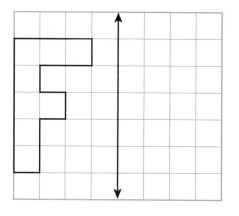

7. a translation along the line

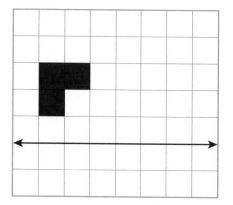

Draw the figure that comes next in the series.

8.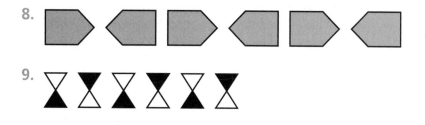

9.

Class Activity

Name _____ Date _____

▶ Grid Paper

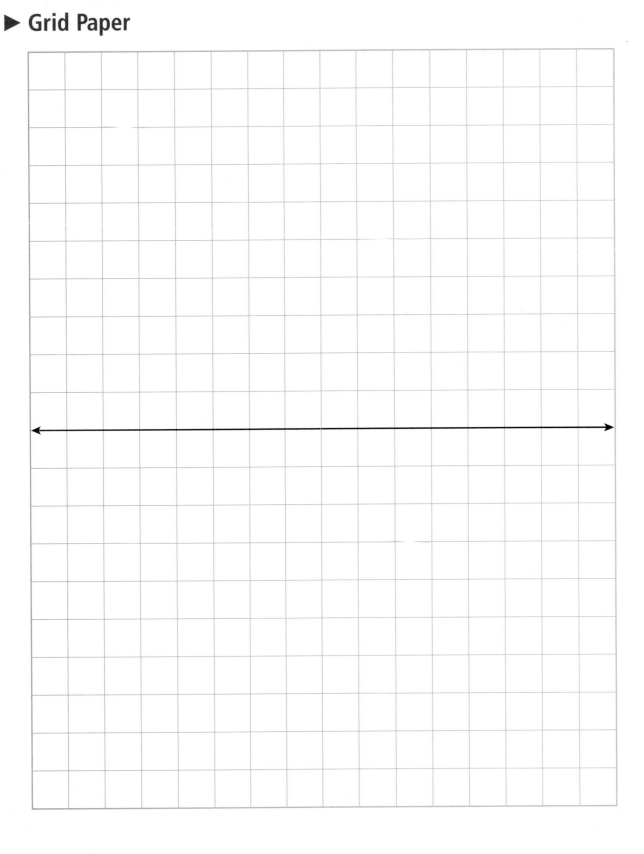

Explore Transformations

Name _____   **Date** _____

▶ **Cutouts**

Cut out each figure.

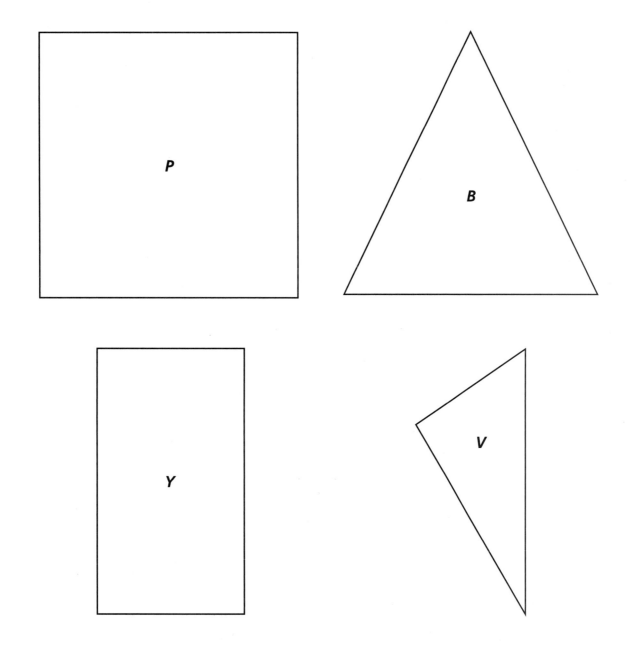

Explore Transformations

Dear Family,

In our math class, we are studying how the position of a shape can be changed. Changing the position of a shape is called a *transformation*. Examples of transformations are shown below.

Transformations

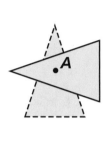

Rotation
(turn)

Reflection
(flip)

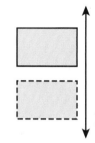

Translation
(slide)

We will also be working with coordinate grids, like the coordinate grid shown at the right.

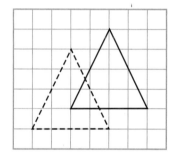

We will discover that the grid shows a translation of the triangle: each point of the triangle has been moved two units to the right and one unit up.

We will also be working with patterns during this unit, and exploring different ways graphs can be used to represent situations in our everyday lives.

If you have any questions or comments, please call or write to me.

Sincerely,
Your child's teacher

Estimada familia:

En la clase de matemáticas estamos estudiando cómo se puede cambiar la posición de una figura. El cambio de posición de una figura se llama *transformación*. A continuación se muestran algunos ejemplos de transformaciones.

Transformaciones

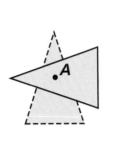

Rotación
(girar)

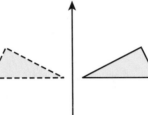

Reflexión
(dar vuelta)

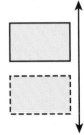

Traslación
(deslizar)

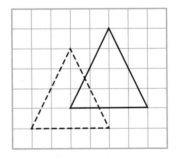

También estaremos trabajando con cuadrículas de coordenadas, como la que se muestra a la derecha. Descubriremos que la cuadrícula muestra una traslación del triangulo: cada punto del triángulo se ha movido dos unidades a la derecha y una unidad hacia arriba.

En esta unidad también estaremos trabajando con patrones y explorando diferentes maneras en que se pueden usar las gráficas para representar situaciones de la vida diaria.

Si tiene alguna pregunta o algún comentario, por favor comuníquese conmigo.

Atentamente,
El maestro o maestra de su niño o niña

Explore Transformations

▶ Find and Draw Points on the Grid

A **coordinate plane** is a grid that has a horizontal **axis** (**x-axis**) and a vertical axis (**y-axis**). You can name any point on the grid using an **ordered pair** (x, y) where x and y are the coordinates that represent distance.

On this grid, the location of point A is (2, 1). On the x- or horizontal axis of the grid, point A is located two units away from 0. On the y- or vertical axis of the grid, point A is located one unit away from the x-axis.

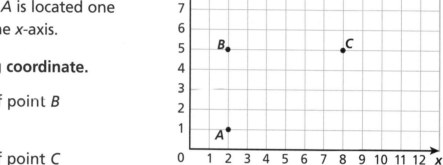

Write the missing coordinate.

1. The location of point B
   is (2, _____).

2. The location of point C
   is (_____, 5).

The first coordinate, or x-coordinate, is the number of an ordered pair that identifies the horizontal distance from 0. The second coordinate, or y-coordinate, identifies the vertical distance from the x-axis.

3. Using your ruler, draw a line segment from point A to point B and from point B to point C. These line segments form two sides of a rectangle.

4. What is the location of the point that completes the rectangle?

   (_____, _____)

5. Draw the point and label it D. Draw two line segments to complete the rectangle.

6. Draw the diagonals of rectangle $ABCD$. At what location do the diagonals of the rectangle intersect?

   (_____, _____)

Class Activity

Name _____   Date _____

▶ Translate Figures on a Coordinate Grid

To translate a figure means to slide it to a different place. On the graph, triangle *PQR* has been translated to the right.

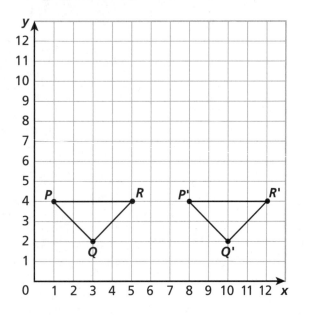

Complete.

7. The distance from *P* to *P'* is _____ units.

8. The distance from *Q* to *Q'* is _____ units.

9. The distance from *R* to *R'* is _____ units.

10. Triangle *P'Q'R'* has been translated _____ units. The distance between each pair of corresponding points is _____ units.

11. Translate each point of triangle *PQR* up 5 units on the coordinate grid above. Use a ruler to draw the new triangle.

12. What is the location of each point of the new triangle?

(_____, _____)   (_____, _____)   (_____, _____)

▶ Reflect Figures on a Coordinate Grid

When a figure is reflected, each of its corresponding points is exactly the same distance from the line of reflection.

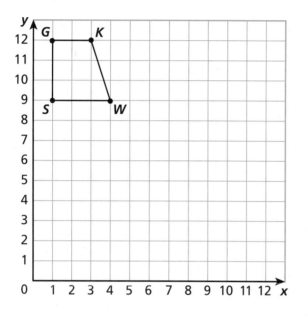

13. Plot a point at (6, 9) and plot a point at (6, 12). Using your ruler, draw a line to connect the points.

14. Reflect trapezoid *GKWS* across the line you drew for exercise 13. Write the ordered pair for the location of each reflected point.

    (_____, _____) (_____, _____) (_____, _____) (_____, _____)

15. Plot points at (8, 8) and (11, 8). Using your ruler, draw a line to connect the points.

16. Reflect the trapezoid you drew for exercise 14 across the line you drew for exercise 15. Write the ordered pair for the location of each reflected point.

    (_____, _____) (_____, _____) (_____, _____) (_____, _____)

Going Further

▶ Plot Points on a Grid

Plot five points anywhere on the first grid, including on the
axes. Be the first to guess where your partner's points are
plotted. Play again using the other grids.

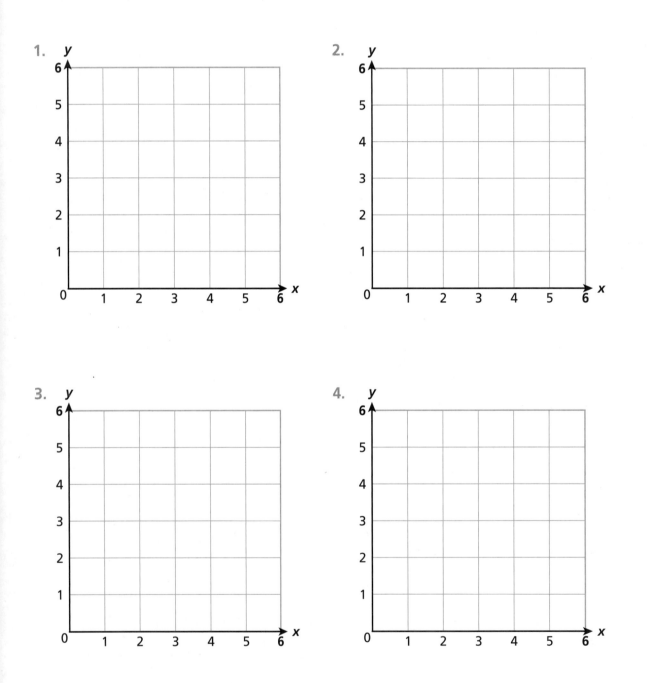

Coordinate Graphs in the First Quadrant

▶ Graph a Function

A **function** is a rule that creates a set of ordered pairs. Each ordered pair of a function begins with a different number.

In a walk for charity, Shayna will earn an amount of money for each mile she walks. The table at the right shows the relationship between miles and dollars.

miles (m)	dollars (d)
1	3
2	6
3	9
4	12
5	15

Complete.

1. Write a rule to describe the number of dollars Shayna will earn for any number of miles she walks.

   _____

2. Write an equation to describe the number of dollars (d) Shayna will earn for any number of miles (m) she walks.

   _____

3. The numbers in each row of the table at the top of the page represent an ordered pair. Graph the ordered pairs and draw a line to connect the points.

4. After the walk, Shayna's mother gave her an additional $5. What equation describes the total number of dollars Shayna earned?

   _____

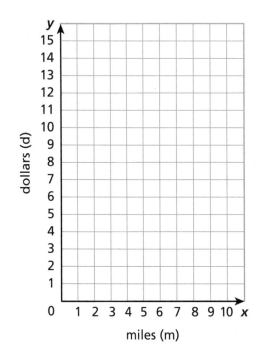

Class Activity

▶ Use a Verbal Rule to Graph a Function

Sometimes we use words to describe a function. For example, *y* is three times greater than *x*.

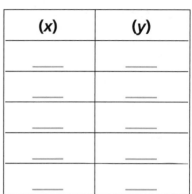

(x)	(y)
___	___
___	___
___	___
___	___
___	___

5. Choose a value for *x*. Complete the table by writing a number for *y* that is three times greater than *x*.

6. The ordered pairs in the table share the relationship that *y* is three times greater than *x*. Write an equation for this relationship.

_____

7. Plot the first three ordered pairs from the table and draw a line to connect the points.

8. Describe how the functions *y* = 3*x* and *y* = *x* + 3 are alike. Describe how they are different.

_____

_____

_____

_____

_____

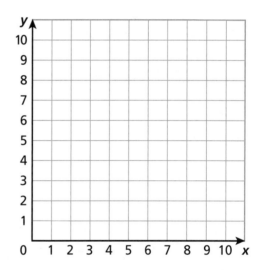

9. Write a situation that the function *y* = 3*x* might represent. Then write a situation that the function *y* = *x* + 3 might represent.

_____

_____

_____

_____

_____

Class Activity

▶ Graph a Function From an Equation

The equation of a function can be used to plot points and draw a graph of the function.

10. Write words to describe the functions $y = 2x$ and $y = x + 2$.

$y = 2x$ _____

$y = 2 + x$ _____

11. Complete a table of ordered pairs for each function.

$y = 2x$	
x	y
___	___
___	___
___	___
___	___
___	___

$y = x + 2$	
x	y
___	___
___	___
___	___
___	___
___	___

12. Plot the coordinates from the tables in exercise 11. Draw a line to connect each set of points.

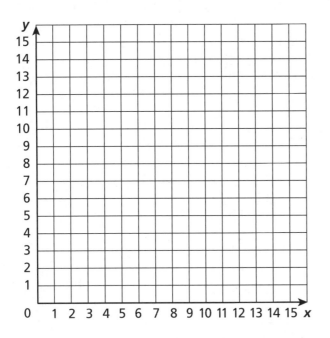

Name _____   **Date** _____

► Use a Graph to Solve a Problem

An earthworm is creating a tunnel in the soil. It moves forward 20 cm each day. Each night it moves 10 cm backward to rest.

Complete the table below to show how far the earthworm is from the beginning of the tunnel at the end of each day.

Day	1	2	3	4	5
Distance (cm)	___	___	___	___	___

1. Graph the points in the table and extend the line. On what day will the earthworm rest at a place that is more than 1 meter from the beginning of the tunnel?

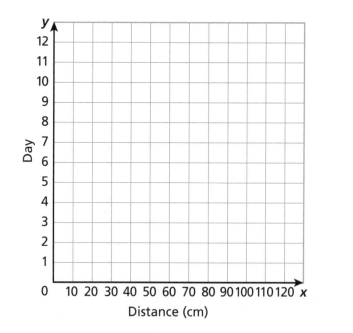

2. The graph above represents one way to solve the earthworm problem. Explain another way to solve this problem.

_____

_____

Vocabulary
negative number

▶ Negative Numbers in the Real World

A **negative number** is a number that is less than 0, for example, −1, −2, −3, −4, −5, and so on.

1. List real-life situations in which negative numbers are used.

_____

_____

_____

_____

▶ Compare Positive and Negative Numbers

A number line can be extended to include negative numbers. The number line below includes positive numbers, negative numbers, and 0.

To compare numbers using a number line, find the position of each number. The number farthest to the right is the greatest number. The number farthest to the left is the least number.

Compare the following numbers on a number line.
Write >, <, or =.

2. 5 ◯ 8   3. −2 ◯ −6   4. 3 ◯ −3   5. −1 ◯ 0

6. −6 ◯ 7   7. 1 ◯ −4   8. −8 ◯ −7   9. 0 ◯ −5

Write the numbers in order from greatest to least.

10. 4, −7, −5, 2 _____

11. −1, 3, −6, −2 _____

▶ Graph Points With Positive and Negative Coordinates

12. Using your ruler, draw a square that has the **origin** (0, 0) as its center. Write an ordered pair to describe the location of each vertex of your square. _____

13. Plot a point at (0, 8). Name two other points on the x-axis that will form an isosceles triangle with (0, 8). _____

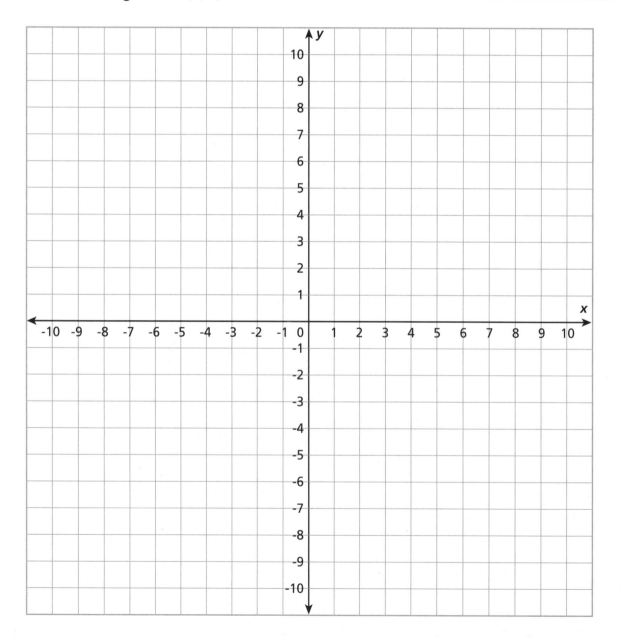

Complete the image and name the transformation.

1.
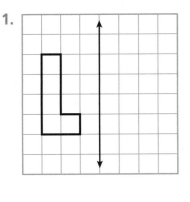

_____

2.
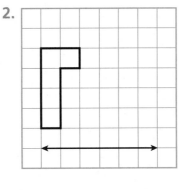

_____

3.
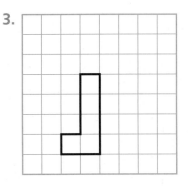

_____

4. Write an ordered pair for the location of point *A*.

_____

5. Draw and label point *B* at (5, 6).

6. Write words to describe the function *y* = 4*x*.

_____

_____

Name _____   Date _____

7. Complete the table of ordered pairs.

y = x + 7	
x	y

8. Plot the ordered pairs from the table in exercise 7. Draw a line to connect the points.

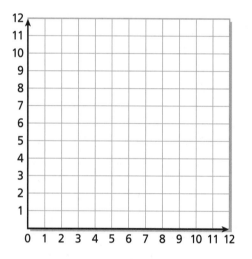

9. Draw the next figure in the pattern.

10. **Extended Response** Describe the pattern in exercise 9. Explain how to find the 16th figure in the pattern.

_____

_____

_____

_____

_____

Class Activity

Name _____ **Date** _____

▶ Fractional Multiplication

Complete.

1. A racetrack is 8 kilometers long. Alex ran around the track 4 times.

   8 taken 4 times = _____ kilometers

   4 × 8 = _____ kilometers

2. Kento ran around the same track $\frac{1}{4}$ times.

   8 taken $\frac{1}{4}$ times = _____ kilometers

   $\frac{1}{4}$ × 8 = _____ kilometers

3. Markers come in sets of 6. Alta has 3 sets.

   6 taken 3 times = _____ markers

   3 × 6 = _____ markers

4. Isabel has $\frac{1}{3}$ of a set of 6 markers.

   6 taken $\frac{1}{3}$ times = _____ markers

   $\frac{1}{3}$ × 6 = _____ markers

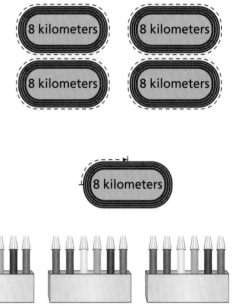

3 sets of 6

$\frac{1}{3}$ set of 6

▶ Relate Fractional Multiplication and Whole-Number Division

Complete each equation chain like the one shown.

$\frac{1}{4}$ of 8 $= \frac{1}{4} × 8 = 8 ÷ 4 = \frac{8}{4} = 2$

5. $\frac{1}{3}$ of 9 $=$ _____ $=$ _____ $=$ _____ $=$ _____

6. $\frac{1}{7}$ of 21 $=$ _____ $=$ _____ $=$ _____ $=$ _____

7. $\frac{1}{5}$ of 30 $=$ _____ $=$ _____ $=$ _____ $=$ _____

8. Circle the expression that does *not* mean the same as the others.

   $\frac{1}{6} × 24$ $24 ÷ 6$ $\frac{24}{6}$ $\frac{6}{24}$ $\frac{1}{6}$ of 24

Class Activity

▶ Practice With Unit Fractions

9. How many times as many fish did Bill catch as Amy?

_____

10. How many times as many fish did Amy catch as Bill?

_____

11. What is $\frac{1}{3} \times 15$? What is $15 \div 3$? What is $\frac{15}{3}$?

_____

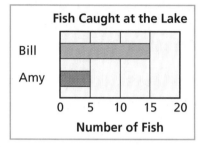

Fish Caught at the Lake

Write two statements for each pair of players.

12. Compare Gina's points and Brent's points.

_____

_____

_____

13. Compare Brent's points and Jacob's points.

_____

_____

14. Compare Jacob's points and Gina's points.

_____

_____

Points at the
Basketball Game

Player	Points
Gina	32
Brent	8
Jacob	4

15. Which are the shortest and longest snakes?
How do you know?

_____

_____

16. If Speedy is 25 inches long, how long is Lola?

_____

Length of Snakes
at the Zoo

Snake	Inches
Speedy	n
Lola	$\frac{1}{5} \times n$
Pretzel	$5 \times n$

17. If Pretzel is 50 inches long, how long is Speedy?
How long is Lola?

_____

Basic Multiplication Concepts

Dear Family,

This is your child's fifth number unit in *Math Expressions.* It is about multiplication and division with fractions.

Multiplying tells how many times we are taking a number. For example, when we take $\frac{4}{5}$ of something, we multiply it by $\frac{4}{5}$ to find the answer. In this unit, your child will learn to:

- multiply a whole number by a unit fraction

$$\frac{1}{b} \times w = \frac{w}{b}$$ $$\frac{1}{3} \times 5 = \frac{5}{3}$$

- multiply a whole number by a non-unit fraction

$$\frac{a}{b} \times w = \frac{a \times w}{b}$$ $$\frac{2}{3} \times 5 = \frac{10}{3}$$

- multiply two fractions

$$\frac{a}{b} \times \frac{c}{d} = \frac{a \times c}{b \times d}$$ $$\frac{2}{3} \times \frac{5}{7} = \frac{10}{21}$$

Division tells us how many of a certain number are inside another number. For example, when we ask how many times $\frac{4}{5}$ fits inside a number, we divide it by $\frac{4}{5}$ to find out. Using the relationship between multiplication and division, your child will discover how to:

- divide a whole number by a unit fraction

$$w \div \frac{1}{d} = w \times d$$ $$6 \div \frac{1}{5} = 6 \times 5 = 30$$

- divide a fraction by a fraction

$$\frac{a}{b} \div \frac{c}{d} = \frac{a}{b} \times \frac{d}{c}$$ $$\frac{4}{7} \div \frac{3}{5} = \frac{4}{7} \times \frac{5}{3} = \frac{20}{21}$$

Throughout the unit, students will also practice the fractional operations they have learned previously—comparing, adding, and subtracting. This helps them maintain what they have learned. It also helps them to see how the various fractional operations are alike and how they are different. It is particularly important for your child to realize that comparing, adding, and subtracting fractions require the denominators to be the same. For multiplying and dividing this is not true.

If you have any questions about this unit, please call or write to me.

Sincerely,
Your child's teacher

Estimada familia,

Esta es la quinta unidad sobre números de *Math Expressions* que va a ver su niño o niña. Se trata de la multiplicación y la división con fracciones.

La multiplicación nos dice cuántas veces se toma un número. Por ejemplo, cuando tomamos $\frac{4}{5}$ de algo, lo multiplicamos por $\frac{4}{5}$ para hallar la respuesta. En esta unidad su niño o niña aprenderá a:

- multiplicar un número entero por una fracción de unidad

$$\frac{1}{b} \times w = \frac{w}{b} \qquad \frac{1}{3} \times 5 = \frac{5}{3}$$

- multiplicar un número entero por una fracción no deunidad

$$\frac{a}{b} \times w = \frac{a \times w}{b} \qquad \frac{2}{3} \times 5 = \frac{10}{3}$$

- multiplicar dos fracciones

$$\frac{a}{b} \times \frac{c}{d} = \frac{a \times c}{b \times d} \qquad \frac{2}{3} \times \frac{5}{7} = \frac{10}{21}$$

La división nos dice qué cantidad de cierto número está dentro de otro número. Por ejemplo, cuando preguntamos cuántas veces cabe $\frac{4}{5}$ dentro de un número, dividimos el número por $\frac{4}{5}$ para saberlo. Al usar la relación entre la multiplicación y la división, su niño o niña va a descubrir cómo

- se divide un númeroentero por una fracción de unidad

$$w \div \frac{1}{d} = w \times d \qquad 6 \div \frac{1}{5} = 6 \times 5 = 30$$

- se divide una fracción por una fracción

$$\frac{a}{b} \div \frac{c}{d} = \frac{a}{b} \times \frac{d}{c} \qquad \frac{4}{7} \div \frac{3}{5} = \frac{4}{7} \times \frac{5}{3} = \frac{20}{21}$$

A lo largo de esta unidad los estudiantes practicarán también las operaciones con fracciones que han aprendido anteriormente: comparar, sumar y restar. Esto les ayuda a retener lo que han aprendido. También les ayuda a ver en qué se parecen y en qué se diferencian las operaciones con fracciones. Sobre todo es importante que su niño o niña se dé cuenta de que para comparar, sumar y restar fracciones hay que tener el mismo denominador. En la multiplicación y división esto no es cierto.

Si tiene alguna duda o comentario, por favor comuníquese conmigo.

Atentamente,
El maestro o la maestra de su niño o niña

Basic Multiplication Concepts

Name _____ **Date** _____

▶ Visualize the Separate Steps

Silver City is 24 miles away. Gus has driven $\frac{1}{4}$ of the distance. Emma has driven $\frac{3}{4}$ of the distance.

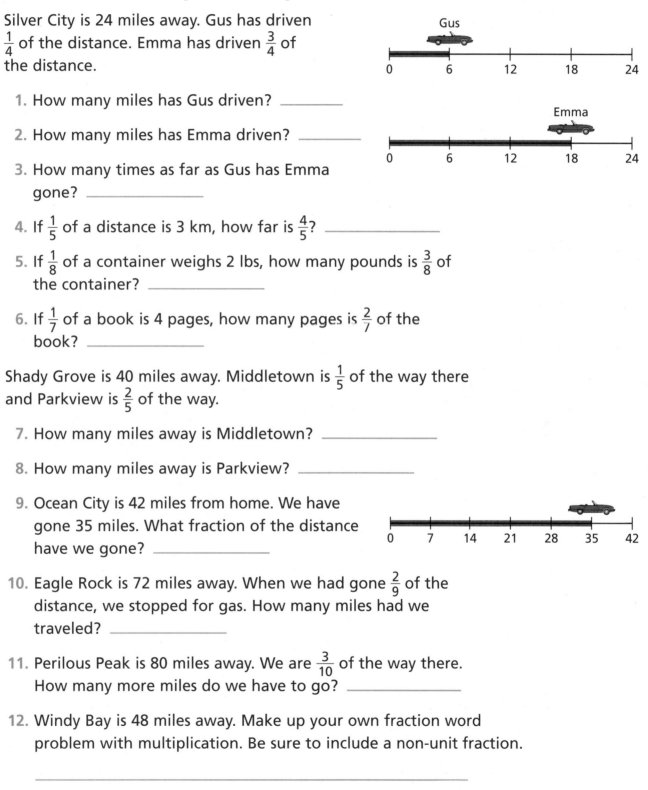

1. How many miles has Gus driven? _____

2. How many miles has Emma driven? _____

3. How many times as far as Gus has Emma gone? _____

4. If $\frac{1}{5}$ of a distance is 3 km, how far is $\frac{4}{5}$? _____

5. If $\frac{1}{8}$ of a container weighs 2 lbs, how many pounds is $\frac{3}{8}$ of the container? _____

6. If $\frac{1}{7}$ of a book is 4 pages, how many pages is $\frac{2}{7}$ of the book? _____

Shady Grove is 40 miles away. Middletown is $\frac{1}{5}$ of the way there and Parkview is $\frac{2}{5}$ of the way.

7. How many miles away is Middletown? _____

8. How many miles away is Parkview? _____

9. Ocean City is 42 miles from home. We have gone 35 miles. What fraction of the distance have we gone? _____

10. Eagle Rock is 72 miles away. When we had gone $\frac{2}{9}$ of the distance, we stopped for gas. How many miles had we traveled? _____

11. Perilous Peak is 80 miles away. We are $\frac{3}{10}$ of the way there. How many more miles do we have to go? _____

12. Windy Bay is 48 miles away. Make up your own fraction word problem with multiplication. Be sure to include a non-unit fraction.

_____

_____

Class Activity

▶ Practice Multiplication With Fractions

Solve the problem pairs.

13. $\frac{1}{3}$ of 18 = _____

    $\frac{2}{3}$ of 18 = _____

14. $\frac{1}{4}$ × 32 = _____

    $\frac{3}{4}$ × 32 = _____

15. $\frac{1}{9}$ × 27 = _____

    $\frac{4}{9}$ × 27 = _____

16. $\frac{1}{6}$ × 42 = _____

    $\frac{5}{6}$ × 42 = _____

17. **Circle the one that does *not* mean the same as the others.**

$\frac{2}{3}$ × 21 $\frac{2}{3}$ of 21   ($\frac{1}{3}$ of 21) + ($\frac{1}{3}$ of 21)

$\frac{2}{3}$ + 21 $\frac{21}{3}$ + $\frac{21}{3}$ ($\frac{1}{3}$ of 21) × 2

Use the table to answer each question.

18. Which building is the tallest? Which is the shortest? How do you know?

    _____

    _____

    _____

Building	Number of Stories
Bank	n
Bus station	$\frac{1}{6}$ × n
Sport shop	$\frac{5}{6}$ × n
Hotel	6 × n

The bus station is 2 stories tall.

19. How many stories does the sport shop have? _____

20. How many stories does the bank have? _____

The bank is 5 stories tall.

21. How many stories tall is the hotel? _____

The hotel is 36 stories tall.

22. How many stories does the bank have? _____

23. How many stories does the bus station have? _____

24. How many stories does the sport shop have? _____

Multiplication With Non-Unit Fractions

Name _____ **Date** _____

▶ Visualize Fractional Answers

Farmer Hanson, Farmer Diaz, and Farmer Smith each have 3 acres of land. They each plowed $\frac{1}{5}$ of their fields.

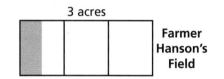

3 acres

Farmer Hanson's Field

1. Can we tell from the picture how many acres Farmer Hanson plowed? Why or why not?

_____

_____

2. Farmer Smith plowed $\frac{1}{5}$ of each acre. Can we tell from the picture how many acres she plowed? Explain.

_____

_____

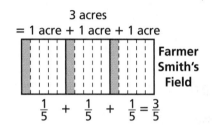

3 acres
= 1 acre + 1 acre + 1 acre

Farmer Smith's Field

$\frac{1}{5} + \frac{1}{5} + \frac{1}{5} = \frac{3}{5}$

3. How can we tell from Farmer Diaz's field that $\frac{1}{5}$ of each acre added together is the same as $\frac{1}{5}$ of the whole field?

_____

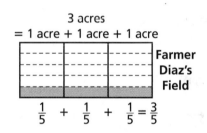

3 acres
= 1 acre + 1 acre + 1 acre

Farmer Diaz's Field

$\frac{1}{5} + \frac{1}{5} + \frac{1}{5} = \frac{3}{5}$

4. Why is $\frac{1}{5}$ of 3 acres the same as $3 \times \frac{1}{5}$?

_____

_____

5. Farmer Belinsky has 7 acres of land. He plowed $\frac{1}{8}$ of each acre. How many acres did he plow altogether?

_____

6. Farmer Davis has 4 acres of land. He plowed $\frac{1}{3}$ of the field. How many acres did he plow?

_____

Solve.

Show your work.

7. Tess practices the flute $\frac{1}{6}$ hour each day. This week she practiced 5 days. How many hours did she practice this week?

Class Activity

▶ Multiply by a Non-Unit Fraction

8. Circle the one that does not mean the same as the others.

$\frac{1}{4}$ of 3 $\frac{1}{4} \times 3$ $4 \times \frac{1}{3}$ $\frac{1}{4} + \frac{1}{4} + \frac{1}{4}$ $3 \times \frac{1}{4}$

Use the number lines to multiply.

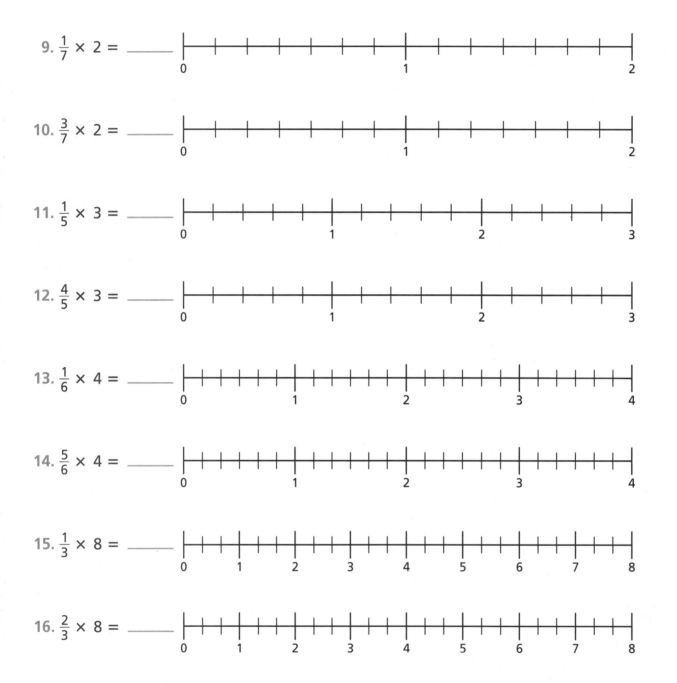

9. $\frac{1}{7} \times 2 =$ _____

10. $\frac{3}{7} \times 2 =$ _____

11. $\frac{1}{5} \times 3 =$ _____

12. $\frac{4}{5} \times 3 =$ _____

13. $\frac{1}{6} \times 4 =$ _____

14. $\frac{5}{6} \times 4 =$ _____

15. $\frac{1}{3} \times 8 =$ _____

16. $\frac{2}{3} \times 8 =$ _____

Multiplication With Fractional Solutions

Name _____ **Date** _____

▶ Simplify and Multiply Fractions

Multiply. Simplify first if you can.

1. $\frac{2}{3} \times 30 =$ _____

2. $\frac{2}{5} \times 35 =$ _____

3. $\frac{5}{6} \times 4 =$ _____

4. $\frac{7}{16} \times 8 =$ _____

5. $\frac{7}{20} \times \frac{5}{14} =$ _____

6. $\frac{2}{16} \times \frac{4}{21} =$ _____

7. $\frac{9}{10} \times \frac{7}{10} =$ _____

8. $\frac{7}{15} \times \frac{10}{21} =$ _____

9. $\frac{5}{24} \times \frac{6}{25} =$ _____

10. $\frac{5}{8} \times \frac{32}{45} =$ _____

11. $\frac{8}{49} \times \frac{7}{10} =$ _____

12. $\frac{7}{25} \times \frac{3}{4} =$ _____

13. Circle the fraction that does not mean the same as the others.

$\frac{3}{9}$ $\frac{1}{3}$ $\frac{8}{24}$ $\frac{10}{30}$ $\frac{6}{18}$ $\frac{9}{36}$ $\frac{20}{60}$

Class Activity

Name _____ **Date** _____

▶ Problem-Solving Situations

Solve.

Show your work.

14. In the Fireside Ski Shop, $\frac{11}{28}$ of the ski caps have tassels. Of the caps with tassels, $\frac{7}{11}$ are blue. What fraction of the caps in the shop are blue with tassels?

_____

15. In the shop, $\frac{27}{32}$ of the jackets have zippers. Of the jackets with zippers, $\frac{8}{9}$ have hoods. What fraction of the jackets in the shop have both zippers and hoods?

_____

16. Five of the 16 workers in the shop know how to ski. $\frac{1}{5}$ of those who can ski know how to snowboard. What fraction of the workers can ski and snowboard?

_____

▶ The Puzzled Penguin

Dear Math Students,

I have a string that is $\frac{3}{4}$ of a yard long. I need to take $\frac{7}{12}$ of it. You can see how I solved the problem at the right.

$$\frac{7}{12} \times \frac{3}{4} = \frac{7 \times 3}{12 \times 4} = \frac{21}{3} = 7 \text{ yd}$$

$$3 \times 1$$

Now I'm wondering about my answer. When you take a fraction of a fraction, you should get a smaller fraction. But my answer is larger. What mistake did I make? How do I correct it?

I simplified by changing 12 × 4 to 3 × 1.

The Puzzled Penguin

17. Write a response to the Puzzled Penguin.

_____

_____

_____

_____

Multiplication Strategies

Class Activity

Name _____ Date _____

► Compare Multiplication and Addition

These fraction strips show how we add and multiply fractions.

Add

| $\frac{1}{5}$ | $\frac{1}{5}$ | $\frac{1}{5}$ | $\frac{1}{5}$ | $\frac{1}{5}$ |

$\frac{3}{5} + \frac{2}{5} = \frac{5}{5}$

Take $\frac{2}{5}$ of the whole

Multiply

$\frac{3}{5} \times \frac{2}{5} = \frac{6}{25}$

Then take $\frac{3}{5}$ of each fifth.

1. Which problem above has the greater answer? How do you know?

   _____

2. Tell which of these questions will have the greater answer. Solve each one.

   $\frac{3}{7} + \frac{2}{7} =$ _____ $\frac{3}{7} \times \frac{2}{7} =$ _____

3. If the denominators are different, can you still tell which answer will be greater? Circle your answer, then solve to check.

   yes   **no**

   $\frac{3}{4} + \frac{1}{6} =$ _____ $\frac{3}{4} \times \frac{1}{6} =$ _____

► Compare Fractional and Whole-Number Operations

Circle each expression with an answer less than the original number. Put a box around each with an answer greater than the original number.

		a and *b* are whole numbers greater than 1.
4. $a + b$	5. $a - b$	6. $a \times b$
7. $\frac{a}{b} + \frac{c}{d}$	8. $\frac{a}{b} - \frac{c}{d}$	9. $\frac{a}{b} \times \frac{c}{d}$

a and *b* are whole numbers greater than 1.

All of the fractions are less than 1.

10. How is multiplying fractions different from multiplying whole numbers?

    _____

    _____

Class Activity

Name _____ Date _____

Vocabulary
commutative property

▶ Word Problems With Mixed Operations

Amber, a very fit snail, moved $\frac{7}{9}$ yard in an hour. She challenged the other snails to try to do better.

Write how far each snail went. Show your work.

11. Willy moved $\frac{4}{5}$ as far as Amber. _____

12. Dusty went $\frac{1}{3}$ of a yard less than Amber. _____

13. Pearl went twice as far as Amber. _____

14. Casey moved $\frac{4}{9}$ of a yard more than Amber. _____

15. Minnie moved half as far as Amber. _____

16. Make up your own question about another snail, Shelly. Ask a classmate to solve it.

_____

_____

▶ The Commutative Property and Fractions

Does $\frac{a}{b} \times \frac{c}{d} = \frac{c}{d} \times \frac{a}{b}$? This relationship is known as the **commutative property**. Look at the proof below.

$$\frac{a}{b} \times \frac{c}{d} \quad = \quad \frac{a \times c}{b \times d} \quad = \quad \frac{c \times a}{d \times b} \quad = \quad \frac{c}{d} \times \frac{a}{b}$$

Problem   Step 1   Step 2   Step 3

17. Explain why each step is true.

Step 1 _____

_____

Step 2 _____

_____

Step 3 _____

_____

Relate Fractional Operations

Name _____

Date _____

▶ Investigate Decimal Patterns

These number lines show decimal equivalents for some common fractions. Discuss patterns you see.

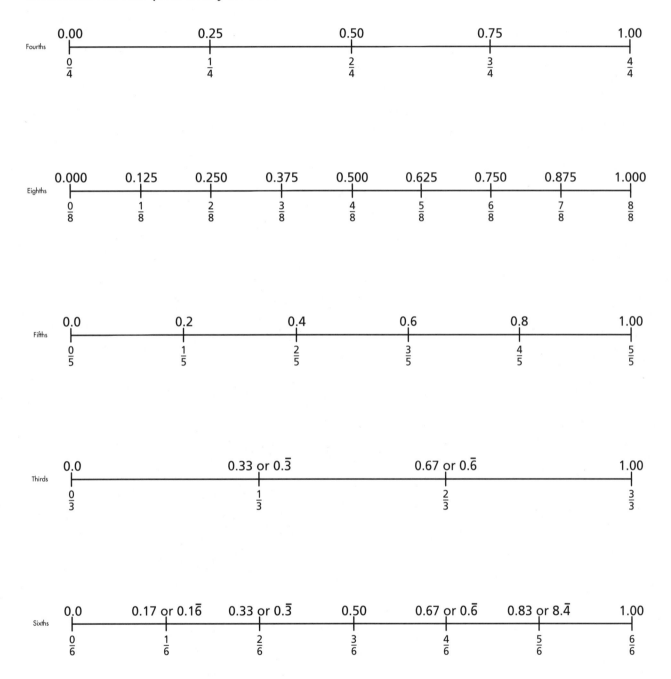

Find Decimal Equivalents of Fractions **351**

Name _____ **Date** _____

Going Further

▶ Problems With Fractions and Decimals

Some problems use both fractions and decimals. Converting the fractions to decimals can sometimes make it easier to compare or work with the numbers.

Solve.

Show your work.

1. Malcolm made $\frac{2}{7}$ of his free throws this year. His friend Darius made 0.31 of his free throws. Who has a better free-throw record this year?

   _____

2. Zoe made $1,000 last year and saved $\frac{7}{8}$ of it. This year she also made $1,000 and saved $890. How much more did she save this year?

   _____

3. Berta needs $\frac{7}{8}$ of a pint of whipped cream to make a dessert. She has 0.9 of a pint. How much whipped cream will be left over?

   _____

4. The bolts that hold the cables on Trudi's bike measure about 0.12 inches across. She has a set of wrenches in these sizes, measured in fractions of an inch: $\frac{5}{32}, \frac{1}{8}, \frac{3}{16}, \frac{1}{4}, \frac{3}{32}$.

   Which wrench should she use?

   _____

5. Trudi also needs to tighten the axle bolts, which measure 0.4 inches across. Does she have a wrench large enough?

   _____

Find Decimal Equivalents of Fractions

▶ Explore Fractional Shares

There are 4 people in the Walton family, but there are only 3 waffles. How can the Waltons share the waffles equally?

Divide each waffle into 4 pieces.

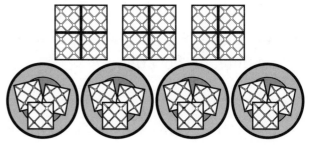

Each person's share of one waffle is $\frac{1}{4}$.
Since there are 3 waffles, each person gets 3 of the $\frac{1}{4}$s, or $\frac{3}{4}$ of a waffle.

$$3 \div 4 = 3 \times \frac{1}{4} = \frac{3}{4}$$

1. Suppose there are 5 people and 4 waffles.

   What is each person's share of 1 waffle? _____

   What is each person's share of 4 waffles? _____

   Complete the equation: $4 \div 5 =$ _____ × _____ = _____

2. Suppose there are 10 people and 7 waffles.

   What is each person's share of 1 waffle? _____

   What is each person's share of 7 waffles? _____

   Complete the equation: $7 \div 10 =$ _____ × _____ = _____

Complete

3. $5 \div 6 =$ _____ × _____ = _____

4. $4 \div 9 =$ _____ × _____ = _____

5. How can you divide 7 waffles equally among 8 people?

   _____

6. How can you divide 39 waffles equally among 5 serving plates?

   _____

Class Activity

▶ Divide by a Unit Fraction

7. How many $\frac{1}{8}$s are there in 1? Write a division equation to show this.

   _____

   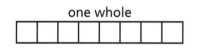
   one whole

8. How many $\frac{1}{8}$s are there in 3? Write a division equation to show this.

   _____

   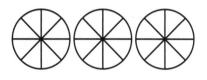

9. Why can you also use the multiplication equation $3 \times 8 = 24$ to show how many $\frac{1}{8}$s are in 3?

   _____

10. How many $\frac{1}{4}$s are there in 5? Write a division and a multiplication equation to show this.

    _____

11. Complete the equation. w and d are whole numbers.

    $$w \div \frac{1}{d} =$$

Write a division equation. Use multiplication to solve each word problem.

Show your work.

12. Olivia made 9 sandwiches and cut each one into fourths. How many fourths does she have?

    _____

13. The 10 members of a hiking club will walk 9 miles. Each person will carry the food pack for an equal distance. How far will each hiker carry the food pack?

    _____

14. Damon has a 6-pound bag of cat food. He feeds his cat $\frac{1}{8}$ pound every day. How many days will the bag last?

    _____

15. Jodie has a box of 12 chocolates. She and her 7 friends will share them equally. How many chocolates will each person get? Give your answer as a simplified mixed number.

    _____

When Dividing Is Also Multiplying

Name _____   Date _____

▶ Add, Subtract, Compare, and Multiply Fractions

The fraction box to the right shows the same two fractions compared, added, subtracted, and multiplied.

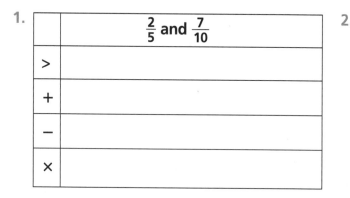

	$\frac{1}{3}$ and $\frac{1}{6}$
>	$\frac{1}{3} > \frac{1}{6}$ or $\frac{2}{6} > \frac{1}{6}$
+	$\frac{1}{3} + \frac{1}{6} = \frac{2}{6} + \frac{1}{6} = \frac{3}{6} = \frac{1}{2}$
−	$\frac{1}{3} - \frac{1}{6} = \frac{2}{6} - \frac{1}{6} = \frac{1}{6}$
×	$\frac{1}{3} \times \frac{1}{6} = \frac{1}{18}$

Complete the fraction box.

1.

	$\frac{2}{5}$ and $\frac{7}{10}$
>	
+	
−	
×	

2.

	$\frac{3}{5}$ and $\frac{4}{7}$
>	
+	
−	
×	

3. How are adding, subtracting, and comparing fractions alike?

_____

4. How is multiplication different from the other operations?

_____

5. The Puzzled Penguin

> Dear Fifth Grade Students,
>
> One of my friends said that he would give $\frac{1}{2}$ of his sandwich to me and $\frac{1}{2}$ of his sandwich to my sister. My sister said, "But then you won't have any left for yourself." This doesn't make sense to me. I know that $\frac{1}{2} + \frac{1}{2} = \frac{2}{4}$. My friend should have plenty left for himself. What do you think?
>
> **The Puzzled Penguin**

_____

_____

_____

Name _____ **Date** _____

▶ Word Problems With Mixed Operations

Solve. Answer in the simplest form.

6. Yesterday Mr. Swenson made $2\frac{3}{4}$ quarts of strawberry jam and $1\frac{1}{8}$ quarts of raspberry jam. How much more strawberry jam did he make than raspberry?

_____

7. Today Mr. Swenson is making $\frac{2}{5}$ of a quart of grape jelly. He will give $\frac{1}{2}$ of this amount to his neighbor. How many quarts will the neighbor get?

_____

8. Mr. Swenson is also making $2\frac{1}{6}$ quarts of cherry jelly and $3\frac{1}{12}$ quarts of orange jelly. He will mix the two kinds together. How much of this mixed jelly will he have?

_____

9. Yesterday Mr. Swenson made $\frac{7}{10}$ of a quart of blueberry jam. His family ate $\frac{1}{10}$ of it. How much of the blueberry jam is left?

_____

10. Mr. Swenson has jars that hold $\frac{5}{6}$ of a quart, jars that hold $\frac{3}{4}$ of a quart, and jars that hold $\frac{2}{3}$ of a quart. Which size holds the most? Which size holds the least? How do you know?

_____

_____

11. Mr. Swenson has jars in these sizes:
    $\frac{3}{4}$ quart, $\frac{2}{5}$ quart, $\frac{5}{8}$ quart, $\frac{4}{5}$ quart, $\frac{3}{10}$ quart

    If he runs out of the $\frac{4}{5}$ quart jars, what jars can he use instead?

_____

Class Activity

Name   Date

▶ Divide a Whole Number by a Fraction

Solve. Use the number lines to help you.

A mountain trail is 6 miles long. A group of runners will race to the top of the mountain.

1. The runners expect to see a marker every $\frac{1}{4}$ mile. How many markers will they see? Write the division equation and the answer.

   Think: How many $\frac{1}{4}$s are there in 6? Look at the number line.

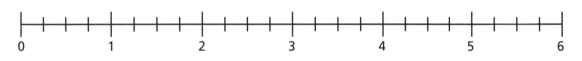

_____

2. The runners expect a water station every $\frac{3}{4}$ mile. Write the division equation and the answer. How many water stations will there be?

   Think: How many $\frac{3}{4}$s are there in 6? Use the number line.

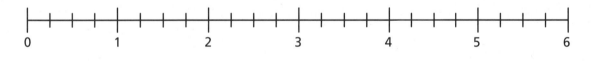

_____

3. How many times as great is your first answer as your second answer? Explain why.

   _____

   _____

   _____

Class Activity

▶ Divide a Fraction by a Fraction

Solve.

4. Alison has $\frac{2}{3}$ of an hour to write postcards. It takes her $\frac{1}{6}$ of an hour to write each one. How many can she write? Write the division equation and the answer.

   Think: How many $\frac{1}{6}$s are in $\frac{2}{3}$? Use the number line.

_____

▶ Solve Multiplication Equations

Find the unknown factor. Rewrite the equation as a division equation.

<u>Division Equation</u>

5. $\frac{2}{3} \times$ _____ $= \frac{8}{15}$ $\frac{8}{15} \div \frac{2}{3} =$ _____

6. $\frac{5}{7} \times$ _____ $= \frac{15}{56}$ _____

7. $\frac{5}{6} \times$ _____ $= \frac{15}{24}$ _____

8. $\frac{2}{5} \times$ _____ $= \frac{6}{20}$ _____

9. $\frac{5}{8} \times$ _____ $= \frac{20}{72}$ _____

These products have been simplified. Use the unsimplified fraction to divide.

10. $\frac{2}{5} \times$ _____ $= \frac{6}{20} = \frac{3}{10}$ _____

11. $\frac{3}{4} \times$ _____ $= \frac{15}{24} = \frac{5}{8}$ _____

Explore Fractional Division

Name   **Date**

▶ Make the Product Divisible

The example below shows how to unsimplify to solve a fractional division.

Solve the equation $\frac{2}{3} \div \frac{5}{7} = ?$

Unsimplify $\frac{2}{3}$. $\frac{2}{3} \times \left(\frac{5}{5} \times \frac{7}{7} \right)$

1. Why do you multiply by $\frac{5}{5}$ and $\frac{7}{7}$?

_____

_____

_____

Divide: $\frac{2 \times 5 \times 7}{3 \times 5 \times 7} \div \frac{5}{7} = ?$

2. In the numerator, $5 \div 5 = 1$.
Divide and write the simplified numerator: $2 \times$ _____

3. In the denominator, $7 \div 7 = 1$.
Divide and write the simplified denominator: $3 \times$ _____

4. Complete the new equation. $\dfrac{2 \times \rule{1cm}{0.4pt}}{3 \times \rule{1cm}{0.4pt}} = \rule{0.6cm}{0.4pt}$

5. What happened to the factor $\frac{5}{7}$?

_____

Unsimplify the product to complete each division.

6. $\frac{3}{8} \div \frac{2}{5} =$ ———————   — = —

7. $\frac{4}{9} \div \frac{3}{8} =$ ———————   — = — =   —

8. $\frac{2}{9} \div \frac{3}{10} =$ ———————   — = —

9. $\frac{2}{7} \div \frac{4}{3} =$ ———————   — = — = —

Class Activity

▶ Explore Division by Inversion

You can unsimplify and divide in one step.

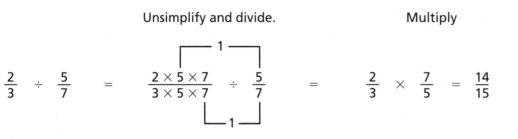

Unsimplify and divide.

Multiply

$$\frac{2}{3} \div \frac{5}{7} = \frac{2 \times 5 \times 7}{3 \times 5 \times 7} \div \frac{5}{7} = \frac{2}{3} \times \frac{7}{5} = \frac{14}{15}$$

10. How is the final multiplication related to the original division?

_____

_____

11. Complete the algebra equation.

$$\frac{a}{b} \div \frac{c}{d} = - \times -$$

12. Use the algebra equation to help you divide.

$$\frac{4}{9} \div \frac{3}{5} = \rule{3cm}{0.4pt}$$

13. Solve the equation by unsimplifying the factor.

$$\frac{4}{9} \div \frac{3}{5} = \rule{3cm}{0.4pt}$$

14. What do you notice about the answers to exercises 12 and 13?

_____

▶ Practice Fractional Division

Complete these fractional divisions by any method.

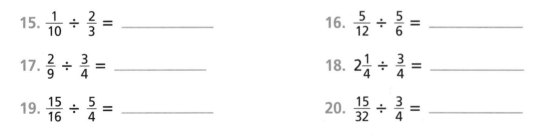

15. $\frac{1}{10} \div \frac{2}{3} = $ _____

16. $\frac{5}{12} \div \frac{5}{6} = $ _____

17. $\frac{2}{9} \div \frac{3}{4} = $ _____

18. $2\frac{1}{4} \div \frac{3}{4} = $ _____

19. $\frac{15}{16} \div \frac{5}{4} = $ _____

20. $\frac{15}{32} \div \frac{3}{4} = $ _____

Name _____   **Date** _____

▶ Solve Fraction Word Problems

The Skyline Skateboard Factory times its workers to see how fast they work. The table shows the time it takes each worker at the factory to make one skateboard. Use the table to solve each problem.

Worker	Time
Kristy	$\frac{3}{5}$ hours
Arturo	$\frac{2}{3}$ hours
Cleta	$\frac{5}{6}$ hours
Tim	$\frac{3}{4}$ hours

Show your work.

1. Tim worked for $3\frac{3}{4}$ hours. How many skateboards did he make?

   _____

2. Today Kristy worked for $3\frac{1}{3}$ hours. How many skateboards and part-skateboards did she make?

   _____

3. Cleta usually works 5 hours a day. How many skateboards and part-skateboards can she make in a day?

   _____

4. Yesterday Arturo worked $5\frac{1}{2}$ hours. How many skateboards and part-skateboards did he make?

   _____

5. Who is the fastest worker at the Skyline Skateboard Factory?

   _____

6. **On the Back** Write a real-life word problem with a solution that involves dividing $3\frac{1}{3}$ by $\frac{3}{5}$. Solve your problem.

Investigate Division by Inversion

▶ Solve Word Problems With Multiplication and Division

Decide whether you need to multiply or divide. Then solve each problem.

1. A turtle crawls $3\frac{1}{3}$ yards in an hour. How far will it crawl in 2 hours?

   _____

   How far will the turtle crawl in $\frac{3}{4}$ of an hour?

   _____

2. Emily has $\frac{3}{5}$ of a ton of sand. She will move it by wheelbarrow to the garden. Her wheelbarrow holds $\frac{1}{10}$ of a ton. How many trips will she make?

   _____

3. Tawanna runs $2\frac{7}{10}$ miles every day. She stops every $\frac{9}{10}$ of a mile to rest. How many stops does she make?

   _____

4. Roberto has a recipe that calls for $\frac{3}{4}$ cup of flour. He wants to use only $\frac{1}{2}$ of the recipe today. How much flour will he need?

   _____

5. A picnic jug holds $\frac{5}{8}$ of a gallon of lemonade. Each paper cup holds $\frac{1}{12}$ of a gallon. How many paper cups, and parts of cups, can be filled?

   _____

6. On the White Gate Chicken Farm $\frac{7}{8}$ of the eggs usually hatch. This year only $\frac{2}{3}$ as many eggs hatched. What fraction of the eggs hatched this year?

   _____

Class Activity

▶ Compare Fractional and Whole-Number Results

In the equations below, *a* and *b* are whole numbers greater than 1. $\frac{n}{d}$ is a fraction less than 1. Answer the questions about the equations.

Multiplication

7. $a \times b = c$

   Will *c* be greater than or less than *a*? _____ Why?

   _____

   _____

8. $a \times \frac{n}{d} = c$

   Will *c* be greater than or less than *a*? _____ Why?

   _____

   _____

Division

9. $a \div b = c$

   Will *c* be greater than or less than *a*? _____ Why?

   _____

   _____

10. $a \div \frac{n}{d} = c$

   Will *c* be greater than or less than *a*? _____ Why?

   _____

   _____

Circle the greater answer. Do not try to calculate the answer.

11. 4,826 × 581   4,826 ÷ 581

12. $\frac{27}{83} \times \frac{13}{72}$ $\frac{27}{83} \div \frac{13}{72}$

Distinguish Multiplication From Division

▶ Estimate Answers

Decide what operation to use, estimate, then solve.

13. Lucy spends 4 hours a week baby-sitting. Her sister Lily spends $\frac{7}{8}$ as much time baby-sitting. Does Lily baby-sit for more or less than 4 hours?

_____

Now find the exact amount of time that Lily baby-sits.

_____

14. Yoshi has a rope 30 feet long. He must cut it into pieces that are each $\frac{5}{6}$ of a foot long. Will he get more or fewer than 30 pieces?

_____

Now find the exact number of pieces that Yoshi will get.

_____

15. Carlos can throw a ball 14 yards. His friend Raul can throw $\frac{3}{7}$ of that distance. Is Raul's throw longer or shorter than 14 yards?

_____

Now find the exact length of Raul's throw.

_____

16. An apple orchard covers 12 acres. There is a watering spout for every $\frac{1}{4}$ of an acre. Are there more or fewer than 12 watering spouts?

_____

Now find the exact number of watering spouts in the orchard.

_____

Name _____   Date _____

▶ Summarize Fractional Operations

17. You have just won a prize on a new quiz show called *Quick Thinking*. The prize will be *n* number of CDs from your favorite music store. You also have a chance to change your prize if you think you can make it better. The host of the show is pointing to the other choices that you have. Which one will you choose?

    _____

18. Suppose that *n* = 6. How many CDs have you won? _____

19. Suppose that *n* = 12. How many CDs have you won? _____

20. Summarize what you have learned about the size of the answers when you mulitiply and divide by whole numbers and fractions.

    _____

    _____

    _____

    _____

    _____

    _____

    _____

    _____

    _____

    _____

    _____

    _____

▶ Choose the Operation

Decide what operation to use. Then solve.

1. Hala can ride her bike $7\frac{1}{2}$ miles in an hour. How far will she ride in 3 hours? How far will she ride in $\frac{2}{3}$ of an hour?

   _____
   _____
   _____

2. Eryn's pet rabbit eats $\frac{5}{12}$ of a pound of food every day. If Eryn buys rabbit food in 5-pound bags, how often does she buy a new bag of rabbit food?

   _____
   _____
   _____

3. Jason practices the trumpet for $1\frac{2}{3}$ hours every day. He stops every $\frac{1}{3}$ of an hour to rest. How many stops does he make?

   _____
   _____
   _____

4. Jonathan can throw a baseball $10\frac{1}{3}$ yards. His brother Joey can throw a baseball $13\frac{1}{12}$ yards. How much farther can Joey throw the ball?

   _____
   _____
   _____

5. Kim bought $\frac{3}{8}$ of a pound of sunflower seeds and $\frac{3}{16}$ of a pound of thistle seed for her bird feeder. How much seed did she buy in all?

   _____
   _____
   _____

6. Casandra's fish bowl holds $\frac{9}{10}$ of a gallon of water. It is now $\frac{2}{3}$ full. How much water does it have?

   _____
   _____
   _____

▶ Estimate Answers

7. Marcus plays basketball for 9 hours each week. His friend Luis spends $\frac{5}{6}$ as much time playing basketball. Who plays more basketball?

   _____
   _____

8. How much time does Luis spend playing basketball?

   _____
   _____

9. Stacey's long jump is 10 feet. That is $\frac{5}{6}$ of a foot longer than Ron's jump. Does Ron jump more or less than 10 feet?

   _____
   _____

10. How long was Ron's jump?

   _____

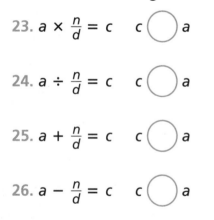

► Practice Fractional Operations

Answer in the simplest form.

11. $\frac{7}{15} \div \frac{2}{3} =$ _____

12. $\frac{5}{12} \div \frac{3}{8} =$ _____

13. $\frac{1}{8} + \frac{5}{6} =$ _____

14. $\frac{4}{9} \div 8 =$ _____

15. $\frac{4}{7} - \frac{1}{3} =$ _____

16. $\frac{5}{8} \times \frac{5}{12} =$ _____

17. $\frac{3}{5} - \frac{6}{35} =$ _____

18. $\frac{2}{5} \times 5 =$ _____

19. $\frac{1}{6} + \frac{2}{9} =$ _____

20. $\frac{2}{3} - \frac{1}{12} =$ _____

21. $\frac{7}{8} \times \frac{2}{5} =$ _____

22. $3 - \frac{4}{5} =$ _____

► Summarize

a is a whole number greater than 1.

$\frac{n}{d}$ is a fraction less than 1.

Write whether *c* is greater than (>) or less than (<) *a*.

23. $a \times \frac{n}{d} = c$ $c \bigcirc a$

24. $a \div \frac{n}{d} = c$ $c \bigcirc a$

25. $a + \frac{n}{d} = c$ $c \bigcirc a$

26. $a - \frac{n}{d} = c$ $c \bigcirc a$

Multiply. Simplify your answers.

1. $\frac{3}{4} \times 6 =$ _____

2. $\frac{2}{3} \times \frac{5}{6} =$ _____

3. Rewrite $12 \times \frac{1}{3}$ as a division expression and show the answer.

   _____

4. Rewrite $\frac{3}{4} \div \frac{1}{3}$ as a multiplication expression and show the answer.

   _____

5. Write the fraction and decimal equivalent for the shaded part of the circle.

   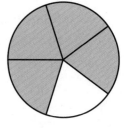

   Fraction: _____

   Decimal: _____

6. Rewrite 0.75 as a fraction in simplest form. Show your work.

   0.75 = _____

Divide. Simplify your answers.

7. $\frac{3}{8} \div 12 =$ _____

8. $\frac{8}{9} \div \frac{2}{3} =$ _____

Solve. Name the operation to use.
Simplify your answers.

Show your work.

9. Kurt swims $1\frac{1}{4}$ km every school day. How many
   kilometers does he usually swim in a week?

   _____

10. **Extended Response** Mila rode in a 12-km bike-a-thon.
    She drank some water every $1\frac{1}{2}$ km.
    How many drinks did she have before crossing the
    finish line?

    _____

    _____

    _____

    _____

    _____

E-1

Class Activity

Name _____   Date _____

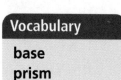

Vocabulary

base
prism

▶ Identify Prisms

Write the shape of the **base** and use it to name the **prism**.

1.

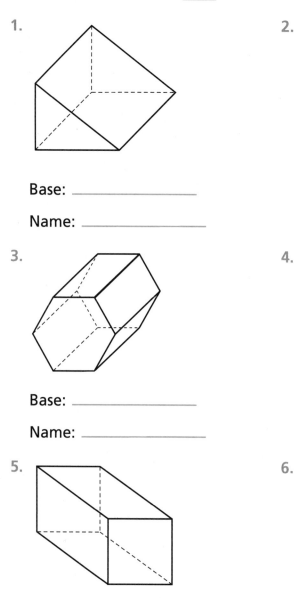

Base: _____

Name: _____

2.

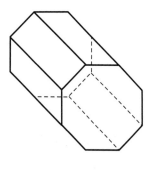

Base: _____

Name: _____

3.

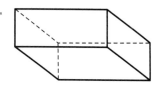

Base: _____

Name: _____

4.

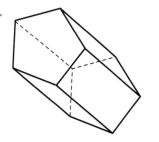

Base: _____

Name: _____

5.

Base: _____

Name: _____

6.

Base: _____

Name: _____

Class Activity

Vocabulary

cylinder
net
circumference

▶ Discuss Cylinders

These are examples of a special kind of solid called a **cylinder**.

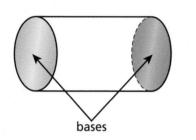

bases

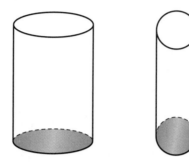

7. List three real-world examples of cylinders.

_____

8. How is a cylinder like a prism?

_____

_____

9. How is a cylinder different from a prism?

_____

_____

▶ Nets for Cylinders

10. Explain how to make a cylinder from this **net**.

_____

_____

11. How is the length of the rectangle related to the **circumference** of each circle?

_____

_____

Prisms and Cylinders

▶ Match Nets and Solids

Match each net in the first column to a solid in the second column.

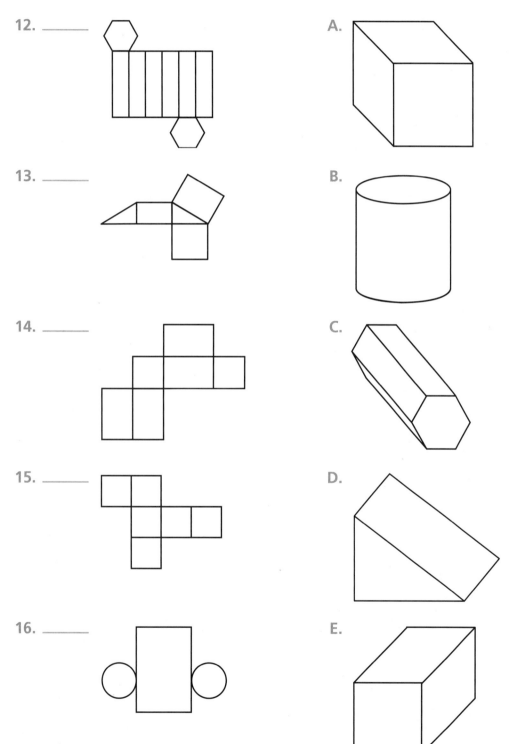

12. _____

13. _____

14. _____

15. _____

16. _____

A.

B.

C.

D.

E.

Vocabulary

surface area

▶ **Find Surface Area**

These nets form prisms. Fill in the missing dimensions. Then find the **surface area** of each prism.

17.

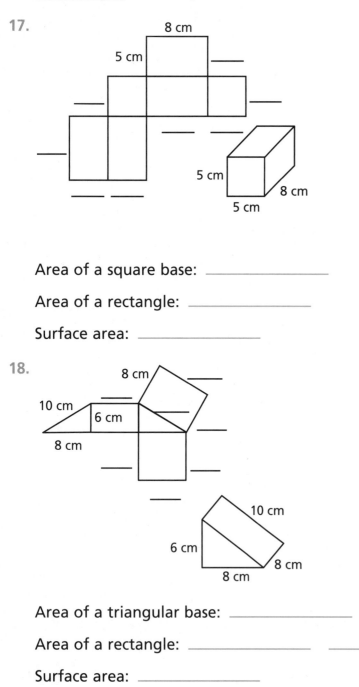

Area of a square base: _____

Area of a rectangle: _____

Surface area: _____

18.

Area of a triangular base: _____

Area of a rectangle: _____   _____   _____

Surface area: _____

19. How can you find the surface area of any prism?

_____

_____

Name each prism and find its surface area.

20.

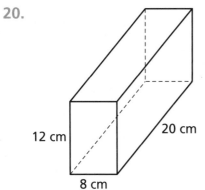

12 cm   20 cm

8 cm

Show your work.

_____

_____

21.

10 in.

10 in.

8 in.

12 in.

12 in.

_____

_____

The edges of this cube are 3 cm long.

3 cm

22. What is the area of each **face**?

_____

23. What is the surface area of the cube?

_____

24. Write one sentence that describes how to find the surface area of a cube.

_____

Class Activity

► Solve Problems

A cube has a surface area of 24 square meters.

25. What is the area of each face? _____

26. What is the length of each edge? _____

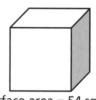

Surface area = 24 sq m

The surface area of a cube is 54 square centimeters.

27. What is the area of each face of the cube?

_____

28. What is the length of each edge?

_____

Surface area = 54 sq cm

One face of a cube has an area of 16 square millimeters.

29. What is the surface area of the cube?

_____

30. What is the length of each edge?

_____

31. What is the volume of the cube?

_____

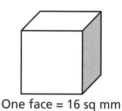

One face = 16 sq mm

A cube has a volume of 8 cubic decimeters.

32. What is the length of each edge?

_____

33. What is the area of each face?

_____

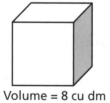

Volume = 8 cu dm

34. Pedro glued together 8 one-inch cubes to make a bigger cube. He then painted the cube red. In square inches, what area of the cube is covered by red paint?

_____

Dear Family,

This fifth geometry unit is about three-dimensional or solid figures. These figures include prisms, cylinders, pyramids, and cones, as shown below.

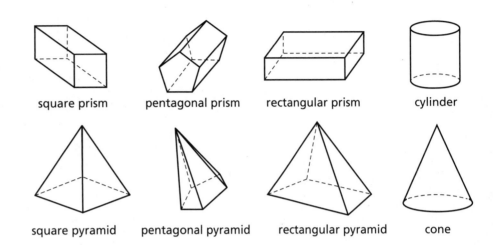

square prism   pentagonal prism   rectangular prism   cylinder

square pyramid   pentagonal pyramid   rectangular pyramid   cone

You can become an active part of your child's learning by asking questions about these figures. For example, you might point to a figure and ask:

• What is the name of this figure?

• What is the shape of its base?

• How many bases does it have?

• How many sides does it have?

• What is the shape of each side?

The next unit involves ratios, proportions, and percents. Your child will be required to add, subtract, multiply, and divide. If necessary, encourage your child to practice these operations. If you need practice materials or if you have any questions, please call or write to me.

Sincerely,
Your child's teacher

Estimada familia,

Esta quinta unidad de geometría se trata de figuras sólidas o tridimensionales. Estas figuras incluyen prismas, cilindros, pirámides y conos, como se muestra a continuación.

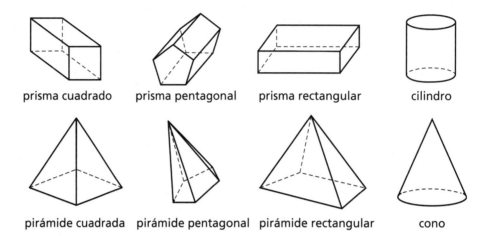

prisma cuadrado   prisma pentagonal   prisma rectangular   cilindro

pirámide cuadrada   pirámide pentagonal   pirámide rectangular   cono

Usted puede pasar a ser parte activa del aprendizaje de su niño o niña haciéndole preguntas sobre estas figuras. Por ejemplo, podría señalar una figura y preguntarle:

• ¿Cómo se llama esta figura?

• ¿Cuál es la forma de su base?

• ¿Cuántas bases tiene?

• ¿Cuántos lados tiene?

• ¿Cuál es la forma de cada lado?

La próxima unidad trata de razones, proporciones y porcentajes. A su niño o niña se le pedirá que sume, reste, multiplique y divida. Si es necesario, anime a su niño o niña a que practique estas operaciones. Si necesita materiales para practicar o si tiene alguna pregunta, por favor comuníquese conmigo.

Atentamente,
El maestro o la maestra de su niño o niña

Class Activity

▶ Make a Cone

Vocabulary

cone
apex

A **cone** is a geometric solid with a circular base. When a cone sits on its base, it has a single vertex at the top, called an **apex**.

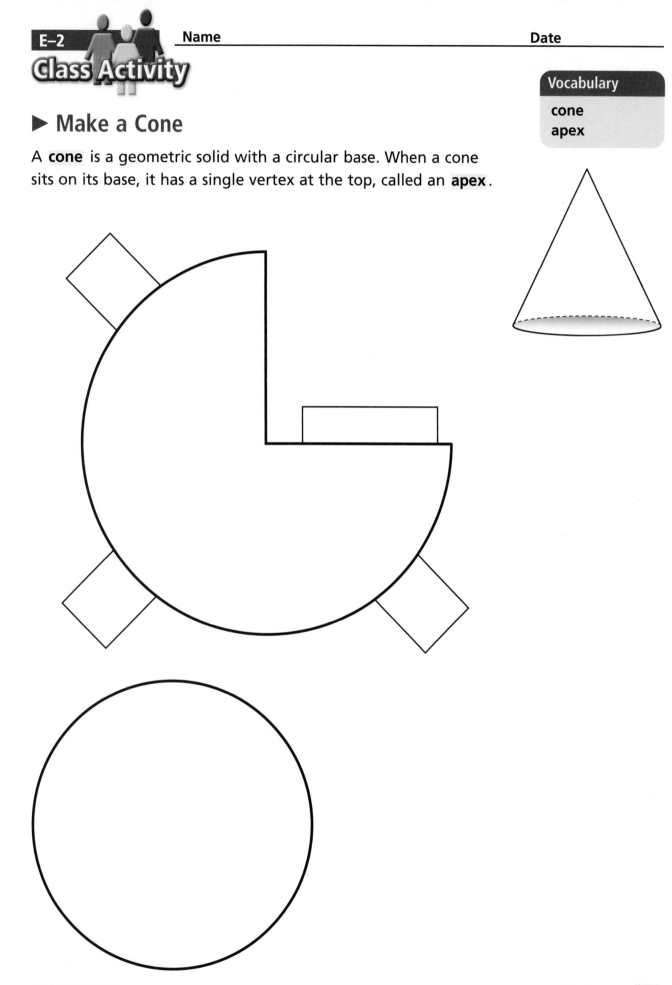

Pyramids and Cones

Class Activity

▶ Compare Pyramids

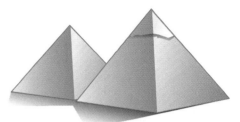

Pyramids have been used in architecture for many centuries.

About 4,000 years ago, Egyptians built huge pyramids of stone blocks. These illustrations show two of the three famous pyramids of Giza. They still stand along the Nile River near the city of Cairo.

About 2,000 years ago, the Maya people built step pyramids to help them track the seasons of the year. This illustration shows the step pyramid in Chichen Itza, Mexico.

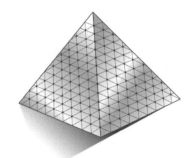

In 1983, Chinese-American architect I.M. Pei was invited to design a glass pyramid for the famous Louvre Museum in Paris, France. This pyramid serves as a skylight for the main entrance to the museum, which is one floor below the pyramid.

A pyramid, like a prism, can have any polygon for a base.

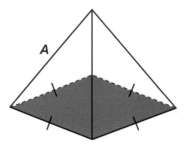

1. What makes pyramids A and B like each other?

_____

_____

2. What makes them different?

A

_____

3. Write a different name for each pyramid.

A _____

B _____

B

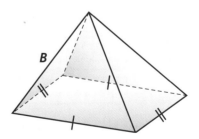

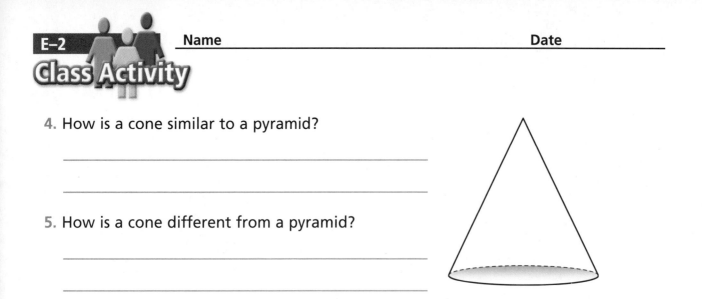

4. How is a cone similar to a pyramid?

_____

_____

5. How is a cone different from a pyramid?

_____

_____

▶ Discuss Pyramids

Name the shape of the base and use it to name the pyramid.

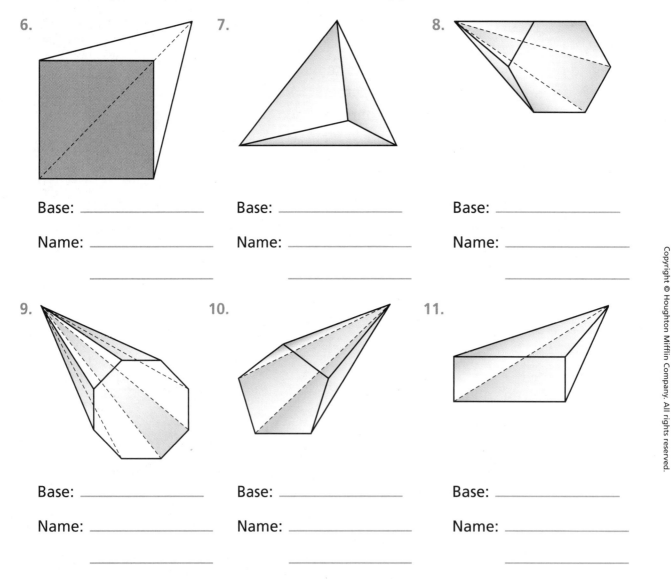

6.

Base: _____

Name: _____

_____

7.

Base: _____

Name: _____

_____

8.

Base: _____

Name: _____

_____

9.

Base: _____

Name: _____

_____

10.

Base: _____

Name: _____

_____

11.

Base: _____

Name: _____

_____

Pyramids and Cones

▶ Pyramids and Nets

Match each net to a solid.

12. _____
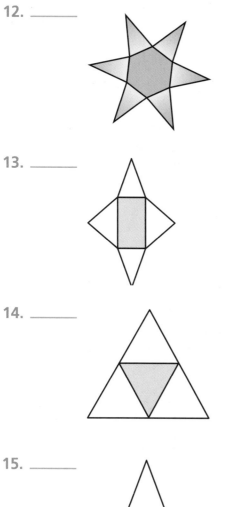

A.
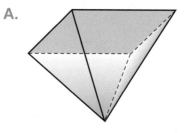

13. _____

B.
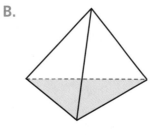

14. _____

C.

15. _____
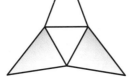

D.
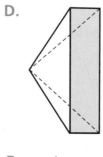

16. _____
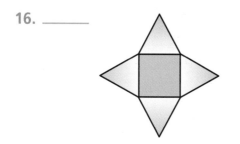

E.

Class Activity

► Find Surface Area

These nets form pyramids. Find the surface area of each net.

17.

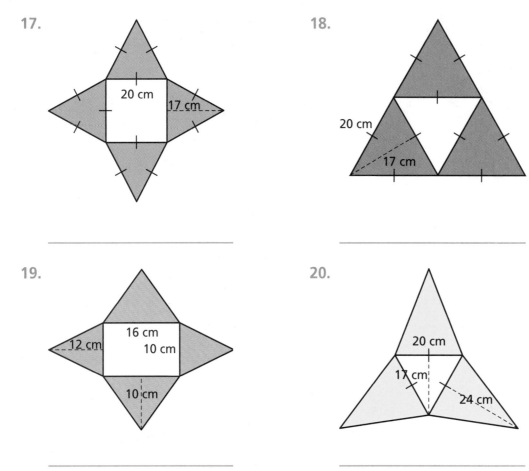

20 cm
17 cm

18.

20 cm
17 cm

_____

19.

16 cm
10 cm
12 cm
10 cm

20.

20 cm
17 cm
24 cm

_____

Find the surface area of each pyramid.

21.

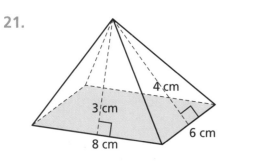

4 cm
3 cm
6 cm
8 cm

22.

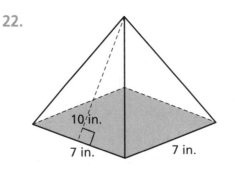

10 in.
7 in.   7 in.

_____

Vocabulary

view

▶ Draw Two-Dimensional Views

These **views** show what a solid figure looks like from the front, side, and top.

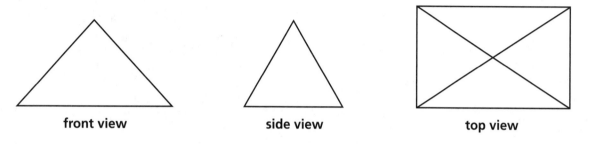

| front view | side view | top view |

1. Circle the solid that matches the views shown above.

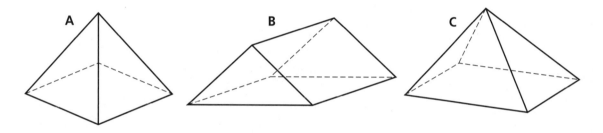

A   B   C

Draw the front, side, and top views of the other two solids. Then name each solid.

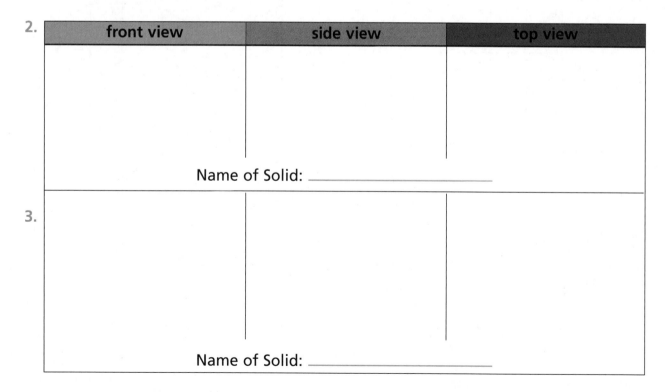

2.	front view	side view	top view

Name of Solid: _____

3.			

Name of Solid: _____

▶ Draw Pictures of Solids

Below are three different views of the figure at the right.

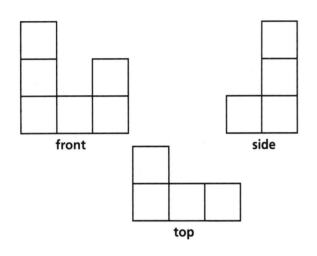

front

side

top

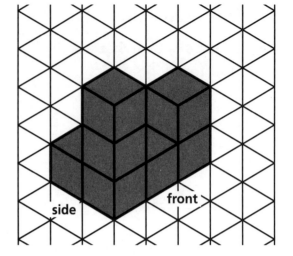

Draw a picture to match the views.

4.

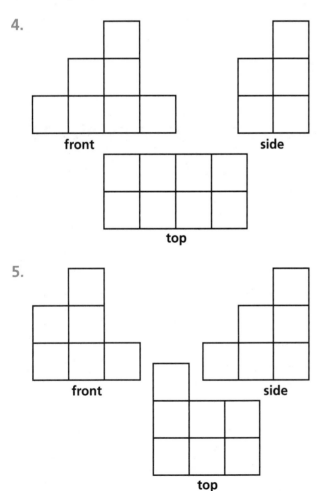

front

side

top

5.

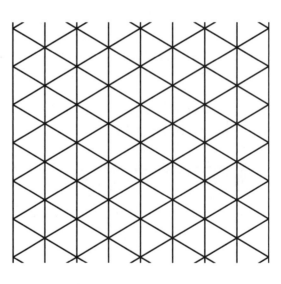

front

side

top

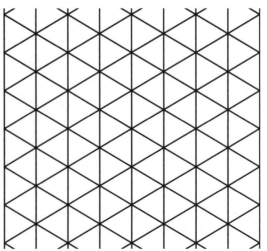

Compare and Contrast Geometric Solids

Name the solid.

1.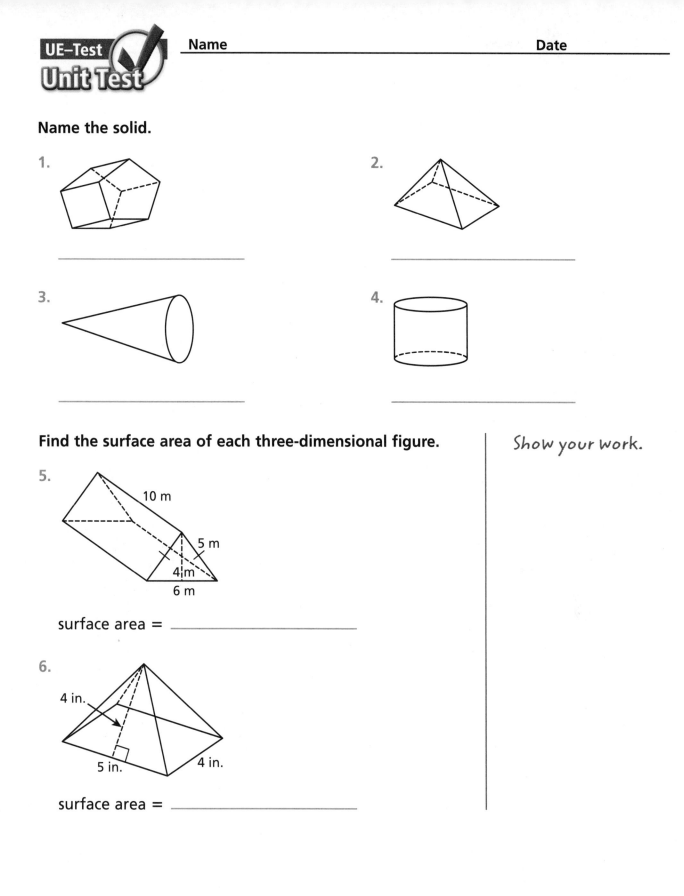

_____

2.

_____

3.

_____

4.

_____

Find the surface area of each three-dimensional figure.

Show your work.

5.

10 m

5 m

4 m

6 m

surface area = _____

6.

4 in.

5 in.

4 in.

surface area = _____

Name the solid that the net makes.

7.

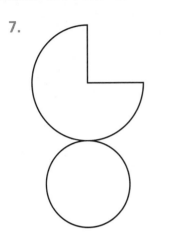

_____

8.

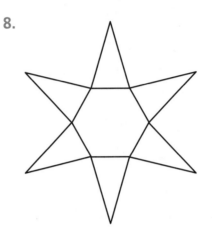

_____

9. Which figure shows the top view of the stack of cubes?

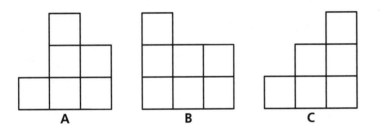

A   B   C

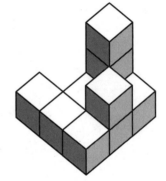

10. **Extended Response** Name the figure.

_____

Draw the views of the figure.

Front	Side	Top

▶ Find the Total So Far

Noreen started to save money. Every day she put three $1 coins into her duck bank. Write how much money she had each day.

On Day 0 Noreen did not put money into her duck bank.		On Day 0 Noreen's duck bank was empty. She had $0.
1. On Day 1 Noreen put $3 into her bank.		On Day 1 Noreen had $_____ in her bank.
2. On Day 2 Noreen put $3 into her bank.		On Day 2 Noreen had $_____ in her bank.
3. On Day 3 Noreen put $3 into her bank.		On Day 3 Noreen had $_____ in her bank.
4. On Day 4 Noreen put $3 into her bank.		On Day 4 Noreen had $_____ in her bank.
5. On Day 5 Noreen put $3 into her bank.		On Day 5 Noreen had $_____ in her bank.
6. On Day 6 Noreen put $3 into her bank.		On Day 6 Noreen had $_____ in her bank.

7. On the back of this page draw and write how much money Noreen would have in her bank on Day 7 and on Day 8.

Multiplication Patterns

Vocabulary

Multiplication Column Table

► Complete a Multiplication Column Table

This **Multiplication Column Table** shows Noreen's savings.

8. Fill in the rest of the table to show how much money Noreen saved each day and how much her total was each day.

Days	Dollars	
0	0	
1	3	+3
2		____
3		____
		____
		____
		____

9. What did you write beside each column?

_____

10. What does the number beside each column show?

_____

_____

► Identify Multiplication Column Tables

These tables show four different ways Noreen could have saved money. Complete each table. Then decide which tables are Multiplication Column Tables and which are not. Explain why.

11.

Days	Dollars	
0	0	
1	2	+2
2		+2
3		+2
4		+2
5		+2
6		+2

_____

_____

_____

_____

12.

Days	Dollars
0	0
1	4
2	12
3	18
4	20
5	24
6	28

+4

_____

_____

_____

_____

_____

13.

Days	Dollars
0	0
1	7
2	14
3	21
4	28
5	35
6	42

_____

_____

_____

_____

_____

14.

Days	Dollars
0	0
1	3
2	5
3	5
4	9
5	11
6	14

_____

_____

_____

_____

_____

_____

Dear Family,

In our math class, we are exploring the ideas of ratio and proportion.

The ratio of one number to another is a simple way to express the relative size of two quantities or measurements. For example, the ratio of the lengths of the sides of this rectangle is 3 to 2.

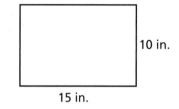

10 in.

15 in.

Another way to write this ratio is 3 : 2.
A proportion is an equation that shows two ratios are equal.

$$3 : 2 = 15 : 10$$

Solving a proportion means finding a number that is missing in the proportion.

$$3 : 2 = 15 : x$$

Your child will learn several ways to solve proportions, including solving Multiplication Table Puzzles.

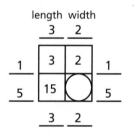

From this puzzle, students can see more easily that the missing number is 5 times the number at the top.

It will be helpful if you can find examples of proportions in your family life and work with your child to become familiar with them. For example, you might follow a cooking or baking recipe and use proportions to make a greater or smaller amount of food. This activity and others will help your child better understand ratio and proportion.

If you have any questions, please call or write to me.

Sincerely,
Your child's teacher

Estimada familia,

En la clase de matemáticas estamos explorando las razones y las proporciones.

La razón de un número a otro es una manera simple de expresar el tamaño relativo de dos cantidades o medidas. Por ejemplo, la razón de las longitudes de los lados de este rectángulo es de 3 a 2.

10 pulgadas

15 pulgadas

Otra manera de escribir esta razón es 3 : 2.
Una proporción es una ecuación que muestra que dos razones son iguales.

$$3 : 2 = 15 : 10$$

Resolver una proporción significa hallar un número que falta en la proporción.

$$3 : 2 = 15 : x$$

Su niño o niña aprenderá varias maneras de resolver proporciones, entre ellas resolver rompecabezas de tablas de multiplicación.

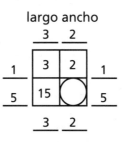

A partir de este rompecabezas, los estudiantes pueden ver más fácilmente que el número que falta es 5 veces el número de arriba.

Será de ayuda si Ud. puede encontrar ejemplos de proporciones en su casa y trabajar con su niño o niña para que se familiarice con ellos. Por ejemplo, podría seguir una receta de cocina y usar proporciones para aumentar o reducir la cantidad de comida. Esta actividad y otras ayudarán a su niño o niña a comprender mejor las razones y las proporciones.

Si tiene alguna duda o comentario, por favor comuníquese conmigo.

Atentamente,
El maestro o la maestra de su niño o niña

Multiplication Patterns

Vocabulary

unit

▶ Use Unit Rate Language

Write each phrase in your own words. Do not use *per*.

1. 4 snails *per* day _____

2. 9 feet *per* second _____

3. 9 books *per* shelf _____

4. $7 *per* sack of rice _____

▶ Use Different Units and Groups

Every multiplication column situation is divided into **units**, and describes a constant group for each unit. Which of these are multiplication column situations? For each one:

• tell the unit and group per unit

• write the situation using the word *per*.

5. In the zoo, 7 kangaroos live in each of the kangaroo living areas.

_____

_____

6. The band marched on the field one row at a time. There were six people in every row.

_____

_____

7. Pedro and Pilar collect snails. Each day they add 4 snails to their terrarium. How many snails do Pedro and Pilar have on Day 5? on Day 10? on Day 20?

_____

_____

8. Last week Ben saw 3 films, this week he saw 4 films, next week he will see 2 films.

_____

9. A hot-air balloon is rising up from the school baseball field. It rises 9 feet every second.

_____

_____

10. A bagging machine was set to place the same number of oranges in a bag. Today none of the settings stay fixed. The machine places 3 and then 5 and then 9 oranges in bags.

_____

11. Every day this week Joanne made 3 of her 7 free-throws during basketball practice.

_____

_____

12. Sandy loves crossword puzzles. She can solve 8 clues each minute.

_____

_____

13. Farmer Brown is driving his tractor down his hilly and flat fields. He can plough 7 rows per hour on the flat field. On the hilly field he sometimes ploughs 6 and sometimes only 5 rows each hour.

_____

Make a multiplication column table for the situations in exercises 5 and 6.

14.

Unit	Rate
Living Area	**Kangaroos**
0	

15.

Unit	Rate
Rows	**People**
0	

▶ Describe a Multiplication Column Story

Decide if each situation is a multiplication story. Write the unit and group for stories that are Multiplication Column Stories. Write "no" if the situation is not a Multiplication Column Story.

1. Each fish tank has 4 snails to help keep the tanks clean.

   Unit: _____

   Group (the unit rate): _____

2. Everyone in the Green family had 2 eggs for breakfast yesterday

   Unit: _____

   Group (the unit rate): _____

3. Tara makes 9 drawings on each page of her sketchbook.

   Unit: _____

   Group: _____

4. Erin puts 3 large photos on 1 shelf and 7 small photos on 1 shelf.

   Unit: _____

   Group: _____

5. Jonathan saves $8 every week, but last week he spent some of his savings to go to a movie.

   Unit: _____

   Group: _____

6. Fred planted 7 tomato vines in each yard he takes care of.

   Unit: _____

   Group: _____

7. Mr. Gomez used 3 boxes of markers in his classroom last week. This week he used 2 boxes of markers.

   Unit: _____

   Group: _____

8. Abby uses 2 cups of flour in each loaf of bread she makes.

Unit: _____

Group: _____

9. Laurie saved the same amount of money each week. After 10 weeks she had $80.

Unit: _____

Group: _____

▶ Write a Definition

10. Write a definition of Multiplication Column Story and discuss your definition.

_____

_____

_____

▶ Identify Multiplication Column Tables

Decide whether each table is a Multiplication Column Table. Explain why or why not.

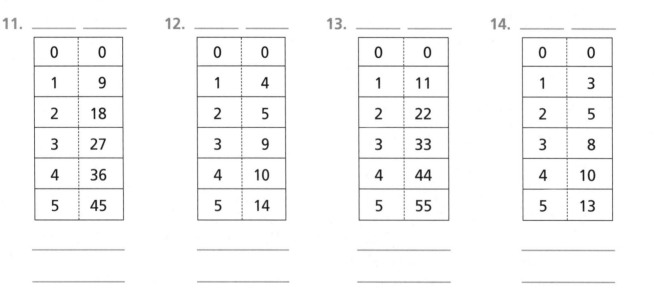

11. _____ _____

0	0
1	9
2	18
3	27
4	36
5	45

12. _____ _____

0	0
1	4
2	5
3	9
4	10
5	14

13. _____ _____

0	0
1	11
2	22
3	33
4	44
5	55

14. _____ _____

0	0
1	3
2	5
3	8
4	10
5	13

_____   _____   _____   _____

_____   _____   _____   _____

15. In your Math Journal, write or tell a different story for each table. Then label each table.

Class Activity

Name _____   **Date** _____

► Linked Multiplication Column Table Situations

Noreen saves $3 a day. Tim saves $5 a day. They start saving on the same day. The **Linked Multiplication Column Table** and the **Ratio Table** show Noreen's and Tim's savings.

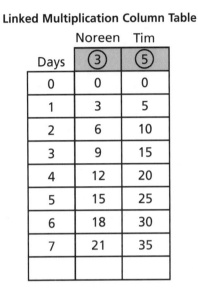

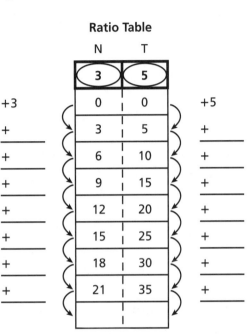

1. How are the tables alike? How are they different?

_____

_____

_____

_____

2. Fill in the numbers at each side of the ratio table to show Noreen and Tim's constant increases.

Use the tables to answer each question.

3. Noreen has saved $12. How much has Tim saved? On which day is this?

_____

4. Tim has saved $35. How much has Noreen saved? On which day is this?

_____

5. On what day will Noreen have $30 in her duck bank? How much will Tim have then?

_____

Class Activity

▶ Create a Ratio Table

Noreen and Tim bought lots of bags of oranges. Each of Tim's bags cost $5, but Noreen paid only $3 for bags on sale.

6. Complete the tables for Noreen and Tim. The linking unit is bags of oranges.

Ratio Table

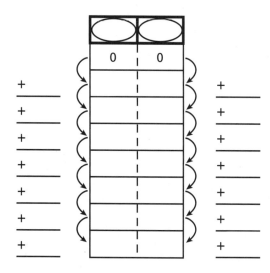

7. How much did 2 bags of oranges cost Noreen? _____ Tim? _____ How much did 4 bags of oranges cost Noreen? _____ Tim? _____

Noreen and Tim plant carrots in their garden. Noreen plants 4 carrot seeds in each row. Tim plants 9 carrot seeds in each row.

8. Fill in the tables about Noreen and Tim. The linking unit is _____.

Ratio Table

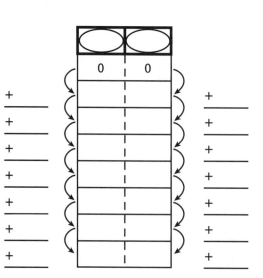

Linked Stories Are Ratios

Name

Date

9. How many carrot seeds will Noreen and Tim each have planted
   after they have planted 3 rows? _____
   6 rows? _____
   7 rows? _____

Noreen makes 5 drawings on each page of her sketchbook. Tim
makes smaller drawings, so he has 7 drawings on each page of
his sketchbook.

10. Fill in the tables. The linking unit is _____.

Linked Multiplication Column Table

Ratio Table

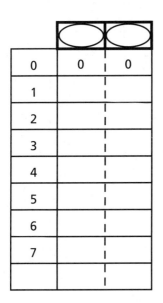

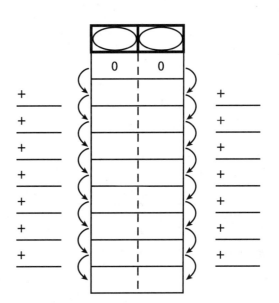

11. What do your tables show about Noreen and Tim's sketchbooks?

   _____

   _____

   How many drawings do Noreen and Tim each have after they
   have filled 3 pages? _____
   How many would each have after 5 pages?

   _____

   How many would each have after 10 pages?

   _____

▶ Recognize Ratio and Non-Ratio Tables

12. Which two tables could be Linked Multiplication Column Tables for Noreen and Tim stories? Why?

_____

_____

_____

_____

A.

0	0	0
1	4	7
2	8	14
3	12	21
4	16	28
5	20	35
6	24	42
7	28	49
8	32	56
9	36	63
10	40	70

B.

0	0	0
1	1	5
2	2	12
3	4	18
4	7	20
5	9	24
6	15	30
7	19	33
8	24	42
9	25	48
10	30	50

C.

0	0	0
1	2	9
2	4	18
3	6	27
4	8	36
5	10	45
6	12	54
7	14	63
8	16	72
9	18	81
10	20	90

D.

0	0	0
1	2	3
2	5	6
3	7	9
4	11	12
5	13	15
6	16	18
7	20	21
8	22	24
9	23	27
10	28	30

13. Why are the other tables not Linked Multiplication Column Tables?

_____

14. Tell a Noreen and Tim story for each of the Linked Multiplication Column Tables above.

_____

_____

_____

_____

Class Activity

Name _____   **Date** _____

Vocabulary

proportion

▶ Proportions and Multiplication Table Puzzles

A **proportion** problem comes from a ratio situation. It uses two rows from a Ratio Table. Two multiples of a ratio make a proportion.

A proportion is written in the form

    28 : 12 = 70 : 30

or   28 : 12 : : 70 : 30

This proportion is read as "28 is to 12 as 70 is to 30."

Here is a proportion problem: Grandfather bought 14 apples for $6. If I buy the same kind of apples, how much will 35 apples cost?

The problem makes this proportion:

    $14 : 6 = 35 : c$

To solve the proportion and the problem, you need to find the value of c.

1. Fill in the Ratio Table for the problem.

2. Circle the rows of the Ratio Table that make the proportion problem.

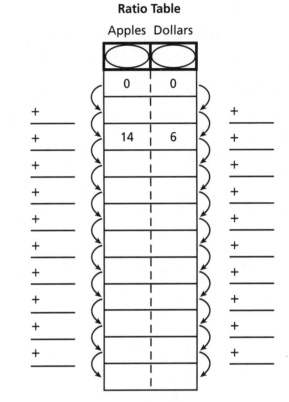

Ratio Table

Apples	Dollars
0	0
14	6

3. Complete the Multiplication Table Puzzle using the numbers in the rows you circled.

4. Write the solution to the apple problem.

_____

_____

Multiplication Table Puzzle

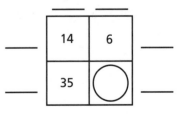

Apples Dollars

14	6
35	○

Class Activity

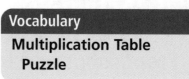

Vocabulary

Multiplication Table Puzzle

▶ Solve Proportion Problems

A proportion problem gives you three of the four numbers in a proportion. You can solve a proportion problem by making a Multiplication Table Puzzle.

Use Multiplication Table Puzzles to solve these proportion problems about Noreen and Tim.

5. When Noreen planted 6 tomatoes, Tim planted 10 tomatoes. If Noreen plants 21 tomatoes, how many will Tim plant?

6. When Noreen had 6 stickers Tim had 21 stickers. How many stickers will Noreen have when Tim has 56?

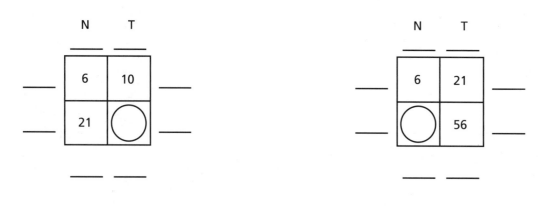

7. Noreen did 72 push-ups while Tim did 32 push-ups. Earlier, while Tim did 12 push-ups, how many did Noreen do? _____

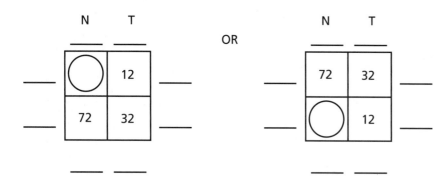

OR

What Are Proportion Situations?

▶ Solve on Your Own

Solve these proportion problems about Diana and Walter. For each problem, complete the Ratio Table and then complete the Multiplication Table Puzzle. Make sure you label the tables and circle the mystery square in the Multiplication Table Puzzle.

8. Diana read 54 pages and Walter read 42. How many pages had Diana read when Walter had read 14?

D   W

| ___ | ◯ | 14 | ___ |
| ___ | 54 | 42 | ___ |

___ ___

9. Diana sold 35 tickets and Walter sold 56. How many tickets had Walter sold when Diana had sold 15?

D   W

| ___ | ◯ | 24 | ___ |
| ___ | 35 | 56 | ___ |

___ ___

10. Diana sliced 30 bananas and Walter sliced 20. When Diana slices 48 bananas, how many will Walter slice?

_____

D   W

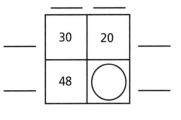

| ___ | 30 | 20 | ___ |
| ___ | 48 | ◯ | ___ |

___ ___

Class Activity

Name _____ **Date** _____

Vocabulary

basic ratio

▶ Think About Proportions

Make Multiplication Table Puzzles to solve the proportion problems below. Tell what you assume about each proportion problem, and then tell the **basic ratio** for each problem. Circle the mystery number in each puzzle and use it to answer the question.

11. Two bands march onto the football field. When Band 1 has 15 people on the field, Band 2 has 6. When Band 2 has 14 people on the field, how many people will Band 1 have?

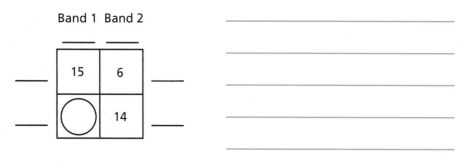

12. Joshua has 32 angelfish and 12 snails. When he has 72 angelfish, how many snails will he have?

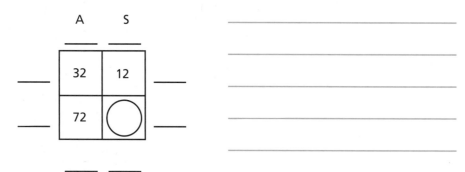

13. Ian planted 25 rose bushes and Ivan planted 30. How many rose bushes had Ivan planted when Ian had planted 15?

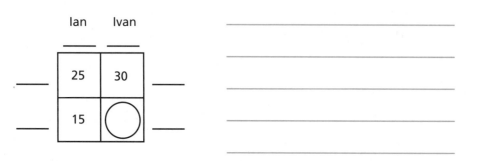

What Are Proportion Situations?

Class Activity

► Solve Problems With Multiplication Table Puzzles

Circle the number of each proportion problem, and then solve the problem. For each proportion problem, make a Multiplication Table Puzzle and write the basic ratio.

1. John can plant 7 tomato vines in the time it takes Joanna to plant 4 tomato vines. How many tomato vines will Joanna have planted when John has planted 42 tomato vines?

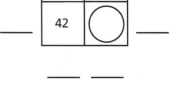

_____

_____

2. Mr. Tally's class uses 2 bags of markers each week. Ms. Petro's class uses 3 bags of markers one week and 2 the next. If Mr. Tally used 14 bags of markers, how many did Ms. Petro use?

_____

_____

3. In the summer Jason's pond had 14 minnows and 6 goldfish. Now it has 27 goldfish. How many minnows does it have now?

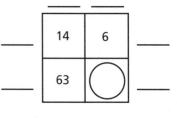

_____

_____

4. Tom is 12 years old. He is 8 years older than his sister Sylvia. How old were Tom and Sylvia 3 years ago?

_____

_____

Name _____ **Date** _____

Class Activity

▶ Make and Use a Ratio Table

Central Middle School has 6 computers and 14 printers.
If East Middle School in the same district has 28 printers,
how many computers does it have?

Here is the solved Multiplication Table Puzzle for this
problem.

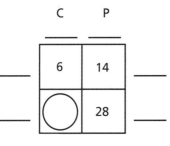

○ : ○
0 : 0

5. Now complete the Ratio Table. Label it, and then
   circle the two rows that make the proportion. What
   is the answer to the problem?

   _____

**Solve the problems below. Make your own Multiplication Table
Puzzles if you need them.**

When there are 6 banana slices in Diana's fruit salad, there
are 14 orange pieces.

Show your work.

6. When there are 28 orange pieces in the fruit salad, how
   many banana slices are there?

   _____

7. When there are 56 orange pieces in the fruit salad, how
   many banana slices are there?

   _____

8. When there are 18 banana slices in the fruit salad, how
   many orange pieces are there?

   _____

▶ Solve Numeric Proportion Problems

Solve each proportion by making a Multiplication Table Puzzle on another sheet of paper. Then write the basic ratio for each.

1. _____ : 32 = 15 : 40   _____

2. 16 : 36 = _____ : 63   _____

3. 42 : _____ = 54 : 63   _____

4. 14 : 56 = 6 : _____   _____

▶ Identify and Solve Proportion Problems

Tell which are proportion problems. Explain why the others are not. Solve the proportion problems using Multiplication Table Puzzles or another method. Write the basic ratio.

5. A bag of 6 oranges costs $2. How many oranges will I get for $10?

   _____

   _____

   _____

6. Cal is 19 and his sister is 13. How old was Cal when his sister was 8?

   _____

   _____

   _____

7. You can make 8 pies from 32 pounds of apples. How many pies can you make from 16 pounds of apples?

   _____

   _____

8. In the zoo, there are 3 flamingos for every 4 ducks. If there are 20 ducks, how many flamingos are there?

   _____

   _____

9. Alice is a mail carrier. Today she is delivering letters on Maple Street. She has letters for people living in houses #4 and #6. If she has letters for house #20, what other house do you think she may have letters for?

   _____

   _____

10. Dana and Sue are sisters. Every week the sisters get an allowance. Dana is older than Sue so she gets more allowance. Now Dana has $48 and Sue has $36. How much will Dana have when Sue has $54?

   _____

   _____

Class Activity

▶ Match Tables to Problems

Write which story from the previous page is represented by each table. One table does not represent a story.

11.

◯ : ◯
0 : 0
1 : 3
2 : 6
3 : 9
4 : 12
5 : 15
6 : 18
7 : 21

_____

12.

◯ : ◯
0 : 0
6 : 2
12 : 4
18 : 6
24 : 8
30 : 10
36 : 12
42 : 14
48 : 16

_____

13.

◯ : ◯
0 : 0
4 : 3
8 : 6
12 : 9
16 : 12
20 : 15
24 : 18
28 : 21
32 : 24
36 : 27
40 : 30
44 : 33
48 : 36

_____

14.

◯ : ◯
0 : 0
1 : 0
2 : 0
3 : 0
4 : 0
5 : 0
6 : 0
7 : 1
8 : 2
9 : 3
10 : 4
11 : 5
12 : 6
13 : 7
14 : 8
15 : 9
16 : 10
17 : 11
18 : 12
19 : 13
20 : 14

_____

15. On a separate sheet of paper, choose one of your favorite Multiplication Table Puzzle situations that you wrote on an earlier day and change it to a proportion problem. Make a Ratio Table for your problem.

Name _____ **Date** _____

▶ Use the Basic Ratio

Solve the proportion problems below using Multiplication Table Puzzles, and then solve them using a different method.

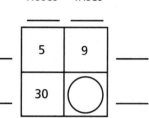

1. Danny filled each vase with 5 roses and 9 irises. How many irises would he need if he uses 30 roses?

   _____

2. $2 : 7 = 10 : y$

   _____

▶ Solve Problems

Tell whether each problem is a proportion word problem or not. Tell why you think so, explaining the assumptions you made. Then solve the problem.

3. Martha and Beth walk home from school at different rates. When Martha walks 35 feet, Beth walks 15 feet. How far has Martha walked when Beth has walked 30 feet?

   _____

   _____

4. If I have 20 blue marbles and 25 red marbles, what is the ratio of blue to red marbles? How many red marbles would be in the same ratio to 8 blue marbles?

   _____

   _____

   _____

5. Maggie bought vegetables at the farmers' market. She chose 6 tomatoes and 9 broccoli bunches. Then she chose 8 carrots. How many heads of lettuce do you think Maggie chose?

   _____

   _____

6. Every day, Mark and Wanda watch *Nature Journal* together, but Wanda has missed some of the episodes. When Mark had seen 7, Wanda had seen 4. When Mark had seen 10, how many episodes had Wanda seen?

_____

_____

_____

_____

Match three tables with the problems that they represent. Which table does not match any problem? Label each table.

7.

◯	◯
0	0
1	0
2	0
3	0
4	1
5	2
6	3
7	4
8	5
9	6
10	7

8.

◯	◯
0	0
5	3
10	4
15	5
20	6
25	7
30	8
35	9
40	10
45	20
50	22

9.

◯	◯
0	0
7	3
14	6
21	9
28	12
35	15
42	18
49	21
56	24
63	27
70	30

10.

◯	◯
0	0
4	5
8	10
12	15
16	20
20	25
24	30
28	35
32	40
36	45
40	50

_____

_____

_____

_____

▶ Write Proportion Problems

Make up a proportion problem for each proportion. Then solve the problem.

1. $24 : 36 = 14 :$ _____

_____

_____

_____

_____

_____

_____

_____

_____

_____

_____

2. _____ $: 24 = 56 : 32$

_____

_____

_____

_____

_____

_____

_____

_____

_____

_____

_____

▶ Practice Solving Proportion Problems

Tell whether each problem is a proportion problem. Explain why or why not. Solve all problems you can solve.

Show your work.

3. A turtle crawled 21 meters in 12 minutes. How long did it take her to crawl 14 meters if she crawled at the same rate the whole time?

   _____

4. At the Party Store 3 big balloons cost $2. How much will 24 big balloons cost?

   _____

5. Every month the public library purchases 10 new fiction books and 7 new DVDs. When the library has purchased 56 new DVDs, how many fiction books will it have purchased?

   _____

6. John and Bill drove to Utah for their vacation. They both drove their cars at the same pace, but they left on different days. John left on Day 1 and Bill left 3 days later on Day 4. John got to Utah on Day 6. What day did Bill get to Utah?

   _____

7. Mr. Munchkin owns a donut bakery downtown. His donut-making machine is pretty good. Out of every 9 donuts, only 2 are not absolutely perfect. He sells these donuts for less. One day, he baked 54 donuts. How many were not perfect?

   _____

8. Two trucks left the dock at exactly the same time and traveled at steady rates. When the first truck had traveled 15 miles, the second truck had traveled 45 miles. How far will the second truck have traveled when the first truck has traveled 30 miles?

Write and Solve Proportion Problems

Class Activity

Name _____   Date _____

Vocabulary

percent

▶ Introduce Percent

1. Circle each **percent** of the 100 pennies.

   1%   5%   10%   14%

   20%   37%   50%   62%

   75%   89%   100%.

   $ 1.00 = 100 pennies

2. Use the percents in exercise 1. Circle each percent of the
   100 millimeters.

   | 1 decimeter = 10 centimeters |
   | = 100 millimeters |

3. Use the percents in exercise 1. Shade each percent of the
   100 square centimeters.

   | 1 square decimeter |
   | = 100 square centimeters |

▶ Relate Percents, Fractions, and Decimals

For each exercise, show each percent of the dollar, decimeter, and square decimeter. Complete the missing numbers.

4. $10\% = \dfrac{10}{100} = \dfrac{}{10}$

   $= 0.10 = 0.1$

5. $20\% = \dfrac{}{100} = \dfrac{}{10} = \dfrac{}{5}$

   $= 0.\underline{\quad}0 = \underline{\quad}$

6. $30\% = \dfrac{}{100} = \dfrac{}{10}$

   $= 0.\underline{\quad}0 = \underline{\quad}$

7. $40\% = \dfrac{}{100} = \dfrac{}{10} = \dfrac{}{5}$

   $= 0.\underline{\quad}0 = \underline{\quad}$

8. $50\% = \dfrac{}{100} = \dfrac{}{10} = \dfrac{}{2}$

   $= 0.\underline{\quad}0 = \underline{\quad}$

9. $60\% = \dfrac{}{100} = \dfrac{}{10} = \dfrac{}{5}$

   $= 0.\underline{\quad}0 = \underline{\quad}$

10. $70\% = \dfrac{}{100} = \dfrac{}{10}$

    $= 0.\underline{\quad}0 = \underline{\quad}$

11. $80\% = \dfrac{}{100} = \dfrac{}{10} = \dfrac{}{5}$

    $= 0.\underline{\quad}0 = \underline{\quad}$

12. $90\% = \dfrac{}{100} = \dfrac{}{10}$

    $= 0.\underline{\quad}0 = \underline{\quad}$

13. $100\% = \dfrac{}{100} = \dfrac{}{10}$

    $= \dfrac{}{5} = \dfrac{}{1}$

    $= \underline{\quad}$

The Meaning of Percent

Class Activity

14. Use a ruler to draw lines across the table from each percent
to connect the equivalent fractions.

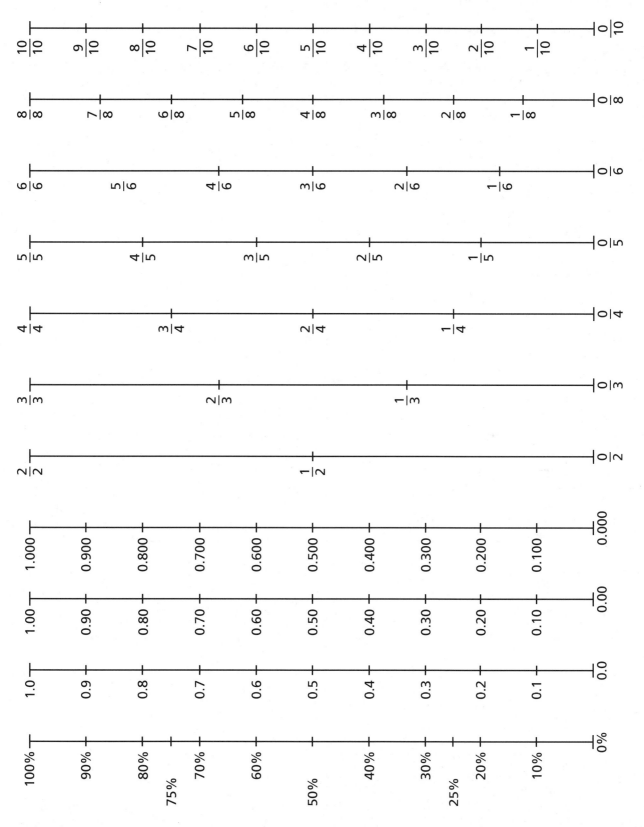

Name _____   Date _____

▶ Practice Percent Equivalencies

15. Fill in the missing percents, decimals, and fractions.

Percent, Decimal, and Fraction Equivalencies					
Cents	Percent of a dollar	Dollars	Decimal	Fraction of 100	Simplest fraction
40 ¢	40%	$0.40	0.40	$\frac{40}{100}$	$\frac{2}{5}$
75 ¢					
	25%				
			0.50		
			0.60		
				$\frac{30}{100}$	
					$\frac{4}{5}$
		$1.00			
		$0.10			
					$\frac{9}{10}$
				$\frac{20}{100}$	
	70%				

▶ Solve Percent Problems With Diagrams

Solve the problems. Use what you know about fractions and percents.

This is 20% of a figure.

1. Draw 80% of the figure.

2. Draw 100% of the figure.

3. Draw 120% of the figure.

4. Draw 200% of the figure.

This is 25% of a figure.

5. Draw 100% of the figure.

6. Draw 150% of the figure.

Name

Date

This is 75% of a figure.

7. Draw 100% of the figure.

8. Draw 25% of the figure.

Here is 75% of a design.

9. Draw 100% of the design.

10. Draw 150% of the design.

11. **This is 150% of a figure.**

Draw 100% of the figure.

This is 200% of a square.

12. Draw the square.

13. Draw 150% of the square.

Solve Problems Using Percents

Class Activity

▶ Solve Numeric Percent Problems

14. What is 25% of 32?

	Percent		Number
Part	$\dfrac{25}{100}$	$=$	$\dfrac{\square}{32}$
Whole			

Why do we write $\dfrac{25}{100}$?

_____

Why is 32 in the denominator?

_____

Solve by simplifying: $\dfrac{25}{100} = \dfrac{\square}{\square} = \dfrac{\square}{32}$

15. 27 is 30% of what?

	Percent		Number
Part	$\dfrac{30}{100}$	$=$	$\dfrac{27}{\square}$
Whole			

Why do we write $\dfrac{30}{100}$?

_____

Why is 27 in the numerator?

_____

Solve by simplifying: $\dfrac{30}{100} = \dfrac{\square}{\square} = \dfrac{27}{\square}$

16. 21 is what percent of 28?

	Percent		Number
Part	$\dfrac{\square}{100}$	$=$	$\dfrac{21}{28}$
Whole			

Why is the missing number above 100?

_____

Why is 21 above 28?

_____

Solve by simplifying: $\dfrac{21}{28} = \dfrac{\square}{\square} =$

17. What is 125% of 28?

	Percent		Number
Part	$\dfrac{125}{100}$	$=$	$\dfrac{\square}{28}$
Whole			

Why is 125 above 100?

_____

Why is 28 in the denominator?

_____

Will the missing number be greater than or less than 28?

_____

Solve by simplifying: $\dfrac{125}{100} = \dfrac{\square}{\square} = \dfrac{\square}{28}$

Set up a proportion and solve by simplifying and finding an equivalent fraction.

18. 75% of 24 is _____.

19. 28 is 80% of _____.

20. 9 is _____ % of 36.

21. 140% of 30 is _____.

▶ Solve Word Problems

Solve the word problems using any method.

22. In Mr. Roberts's class there are 30 children. 18 of them are girls. What percent of the children in Mr. Roberts's class are girls?

_____

23. Andrew counted 20 fish in the pond at City Park. 15 were goldfish and the rest were carp. What percent of the fish were goldfish?

_____

24. A jug holds 80 mL of water when it is full. How much water will there be in the jug when it is 75% full?

_____

25. After a long diet, the dog Lucky weighed 54 pounds. That was 90% of his old weight. How much did Lucky weigh before the diet?

_____

26. Emma saw the movie *The Mummy* 4 times. That is only 80% of the number of times Yoko has seen it. How many times has Yoko seen *The Mummy*?

_____

27. Kevin made 55 sandwiches for the party. 33 of the sandwiches were tuna. What percent of the sandwiches were tuna?

_____

28. Chip has already eaten 320 of the 400 acorns he collected for winter. What percent of his acorns has Chip eaten?

_____

29. In Mr. Smith's front yard there is an olive tree and a palm tree. The olive tree is 12 feet tall and the palm tree is 15 feet tall. The olive tree's height is what percent of the palm tree's height?

_____

6–12 Class Activity

Name _____ Date _____

▶ Solve Probability Problems

Show your work.

Solve each problem using any method.

1. A box of 40 crayons has 10 shades of red, 6 shades of blue, 4 shades of yellow, 2 shades of purple, as well as other colors. What is the probability of getting a red crayon? A blue crayon? A yellow crayon? A purple crayon? Express your answers as a percent.

_____

2. The grab bag at the town picnic contained 2,000 tickets to local baseball games. 40% were Pigeon tickets, 35% were Robin tickets, and 25% were Sparrow tickets. If you drew out 20 tickets, how many tickets for each team would you expect to get? How many Pigeon tickets are there?

_____

_____

3. Peppy the cat sleeps 18 hours a day. What is the percent chance that you will find Peppy asleep at any one time of day?

_____

4. A bushel of apples contains 32 Jonathan apples, 28 Golden Delicious apples, and 20 Granny Smith apples. What are your chances of picking one Jonathan apple from the bushel? Express your answer as a percent.

_____

5. What are your chances of each spinner landing on a dark space? Express your answers as a percent.

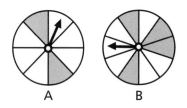

A   B

Of the 5,000 children who live in Garden Town, 4,500 love to eat vegetables.

6. What percent of the children love to eat vegetables?

_____

7. Of the 30 children who live on Green Bean Street in Garden Town, how many probably do not like to eat vegetables?

_____

8. A box of 30 chocolates has 12 chocolate-covered caramels, 6 chocolate-covered cherries, 3 chocolates with nougat centers, and 9 solid chocolates. What is the probability of picking a chocolate-covered caramel? A chocolate-covered cherry? A chocolate with a nougat center? Solid chocolate? Express your answers as percents.

_____

_____

_____

9. Dorothy bought a bag of 500 mixed flower seeds. The bag contained 250 dahlia seeds, 120 daisy seeds, 75 violet seeds, and the rest were forget-me-nots. Dorothy planted 200 of the seeds in her garden. How many of each flower can she expect to grow in her garden? Make a table to show your answers.

_____

_____

1. Circle the multiplication column table. Explain why the other table is not a multiplication column table.

0	0
1	3
2	6
3	8
4	10
5	13
6	17
7	18

0	0
1	8
2	16
3	24
4	32
5	40
6	48
7	56

_____

_____

_____

2. Grandma Jackson has 56 tomato plants in 7 rows of her garden. Complete this statement.

   Grandma Jackson has

   _____ per _____ .

3. Make a ratio table for this situation.

   A fruit salad recipe calls for 7 bananas for every 3 oranges.

   Be sure to label your table.

4. What is the value of *x*?

   x : 27 = 42 : 18

   x = _____

Ratio Table

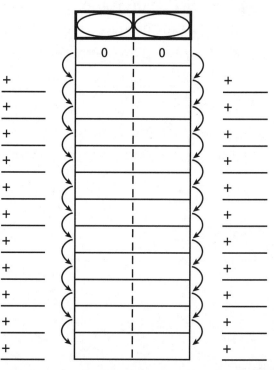

Name _____ Date _____

Complete the Multiplication Table Puzzle and solve the problem.

5. Jerry saved $12 for every $15 that Ellen saved. When Jerry had saved $28, how much had Ellen saved?

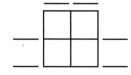

_____

Solve each problem.

Show your work.

6. The ratio of craft books to fiction books in the Springfield Public Library is 3 to 10. The library has 80 fiction books. How many craft books does it have?

_____

7. Every day during October, Ms. Carter fills 3 baskets with apples and 8 baskets with pears. When she has 40 baskets of pears, how many baskets of apples does she have?

_____

8. Al had $75 when he went shopping. He spent 60% of his money. How much did he have left when he came home?

_____

9. A bag of 25 marbles contains 8 red marbles. If one marble is picked from the bag, what is the probability that it is red? Express your answer as a percent.

_____

10. **Extended Response** Write a word problem for the proportion and show how to solve the problem.

$$x : 56 = 6 : 24$$

_____

_____

_____

Vocabulary

similar
ratio

▶ Discuss Similar Figures

When figures are similar, the measurements of corresponding angles are equal and the lengths of corresponding sides share the same ratio.

All of these rectangles are similar.

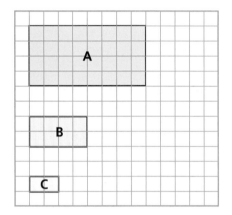

Two of these triangles are similar.

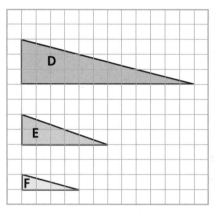

1. Write a ratio in simplest form that compares the measurements of the base and the height.

A _____ B _____ C _____

2. Write a ratio in simplest form that compares the measurements of the base and the height.

D _____ E _____ F _____

Is each pair of figures similar? Circle yes or no.

3.

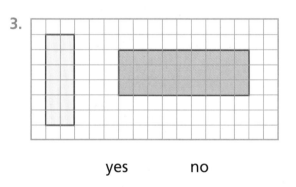

yes   no

4.

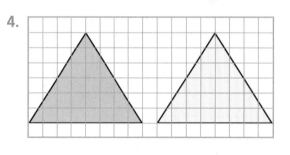

yes   no

5.

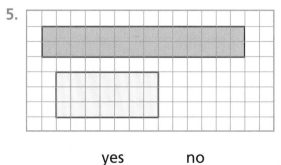

yes   no

6.

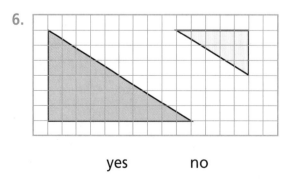

yes   no

▶ Draw Similar Figures

Use each figure to complete the exercises.

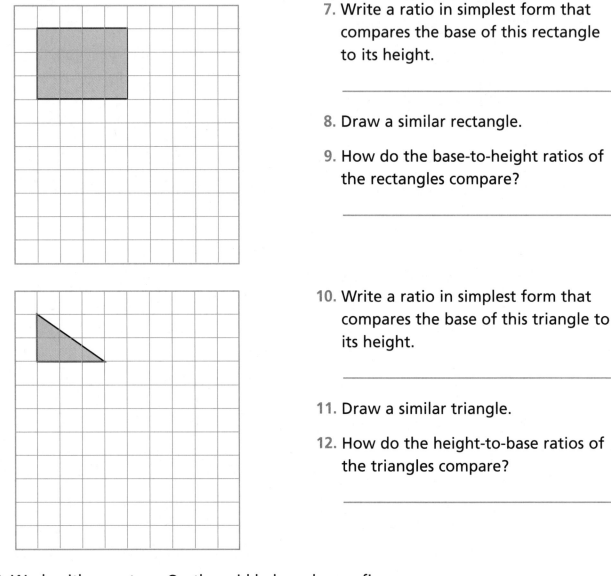

7. Write a ratio in simplest form that compares the base of this rectangle to its height.

   _____

8. Draw a similar rectangle.

9. How do the base-to-height ratios of the rectangles compare?

   _____

10. Write a ratio in simplest form that compares the base of this triangle to its height.

    _____

11. Draw a similar triangle.

12. How do the height-to-base ratios of the triangles compare?

    _____

13. Work with a partner. On the grid below, draw a figure. Challenge your partner to draw a figure that is similar, but not congruent.

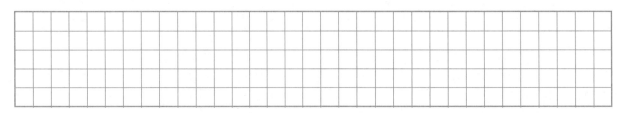

▶ Compare Measurements

When two figures are similar, you can use known measurements to find an unknown measurement.

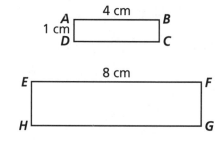

These rectangles are similar. What is the length of $\overline{EH}$?

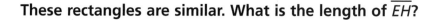

Use Mental Math	**Use a Proportion**

14. What is the length of $\overline{DC}$? _____

15. What is the length of $\overline{HG}$? _____

16. How do the lengths compare?

_____

_____

18. What is the ratio of DC to HG? _____

19. What is the ratio of AD to EH? _____

20. Solve for n.

$\frac{4}{8} = \frac{1}{n}$ or $\frac{1}{n} = \frac{4}{8}$ $n =$ _____

17. What is the length of $\overline{EH}$? _____

Write each missing measurement.

21.

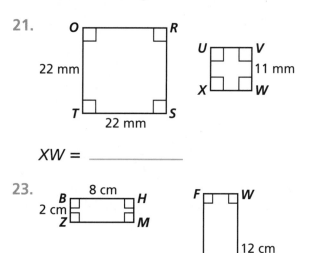

$XW =$ _____

22.

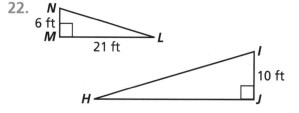

$JH =$ _____

23.

$WF =$ _____

24.

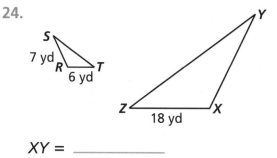

$XY =$ _____

Going Further

▶ Show Perspective

Similarity can be used to show perspective. The smaller a figure is, the farther away it appears.

1. Cut out the similar rectangles on the next page.

2. On the grid below, glue the largest rectangle near the bottom and the smallest rectangle near the top.

3. To show perspective, draw lines to connect corresponding vertices.

4. Glue the third rectangle so that it fits within the lines you drew.

5. Use the lines to draw two other rectangles that are similar to these rectangles.

Similar Figures

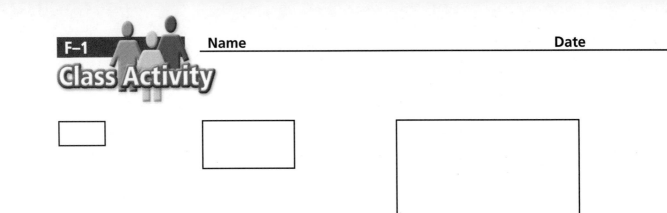

Similar Figures

Dear Family,

This unit is your child's sixth mini unit in *Math Expressions*. It introduces similarity and scale. There are two main goals for this unit:

1. Students will identify and draw similar figures, and use similarity to find a missing measurement.

   • One figure is similar to another if it has the same shape. It may be enlarged or reduced.

   • In similar figures, the measurements of corresponding angles are equal and the lengths of the sides share the same ratio.

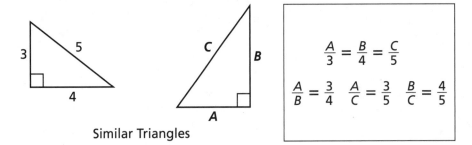

Similar Triangles

2. Students will analyze and interpret scale drawings, including maps, and make two-dimensional scale drawings.

   • In scale drawings and maps, the actual object and the drawing are similar.

   • The scale tells the relationship between the distances in the drawing or map and the actual distances. For example, $\frac{1}{4}$ inch = 100 miles means that every $\frac{1}{4}$ inch on the map represents 100 actual miles.

If you have any questions or comments, please call or write to me.

Sincerely,
Your child's teacher

Estimada familia:

Su niño o niña empieza la sexta unidad de *Math Expressions*. Se presentan la semejanza y las escalas. Esta unidad tiene dos objetivos principales:

1. Los estudiantes identificarán y dibujarán figuras semejantes y usarán la semejanza para hallar una medida que falta.

   • Una figura es semejante a otra si tiene la misma forma. Puede ser aumentada o reducida.

   • En figuras semejantes, las medidas de los ángulos correspondientes son iguales y las longitudes de los lados tienen la misma razón entre sí.

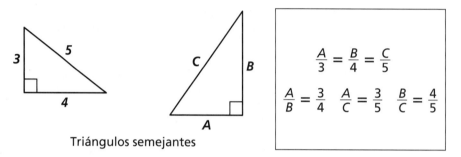

Triángulos semejantes

2. Los estudiantes analizarán e interpretarán dibujos a escala, incluidos los mapas, y harán dibujos bidimensionales a escala.

   • En los dibujos a escala y en los mapas, el objeto real y el dibujo son semejantes.

   • La escala indica la relación entre las distancias en el dibujo o mapa y las distancias reales. Por ejemplo, $\frac{1}{4}$ de pulgada = 100 millas significa que cada $\frac{1}{4}$ de pulgada del mapa representa 100 millas reales.

Si tiene alguna duda o comentario, por favor comuníquese conmigo.

Atentamente,
El maestro o la maestra de su niño o niña

Similar Figures

Vocabulary

scale

▶ Read a Map

A map is an example of a **scale** drawing. On the map below, every inch represents a specified distance. To find the distance that an inch represents, use the scale located on the map.

1. What distance does each inch on the map represent?

_____

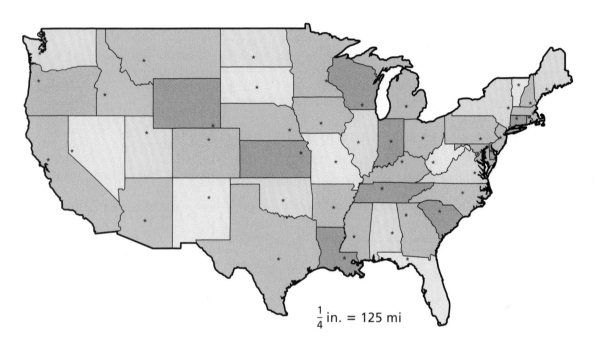

$\frac{1}{4}$ in. = 125 mi

Use the map and an inch ruler to answer the questions below.

2. Choose a state capital and write its name.

_____

3. Locate another state capital and write its name.

_____

4. To the nearest fifty miles, what is the distance between the capitals? _____ miles

Class Activity

▶ Plan a Trip

**Use the map on the previous page and an inch ruler to answer
the questions below.**

5. List four states you might like to visit someday.

   _____

   _____

   _____

   _____

6. On the map, write the names of the capitals of those states.

7. Plan a trip to visit those capitals. Your trip should begin and
   end at your own state capital. Write the names of the capitals
   in the order you will visit them. Which capital will you visit
   first? Which will you visit second?

   _____

   _____

8. Using the map scale and a ruler, estimate the total distance
   you will travel, to the nearest hundred miles.

   _____ miles

9. If you change the order in which you visit the capitals, will
   the total distance of your trip change? Explain.

   _____

   _____

10. In which order should you visit the capitals so that your trip is
    the shortest possible distance? What is that distance?

    _____

    _____

Class Activity

Name _____ **Date** _____

▶ Will It Fit?

A **scale drawing** represents two dimensions, and includes a scale and a **key**. The key is used to explain the scale and what the symbols on the drawing represent.

Use a centimeter ruler to measure the rugs in exercises 1 and 2. Then decide if each rug will fit in your classroom. Write yes or no.

1. To the right is a view of a rug drawn to the scale 1 cm = 60 cm.

   _____

2. This is a view of a different rug drawn to the scale 1 cm = 2 m.

   _____

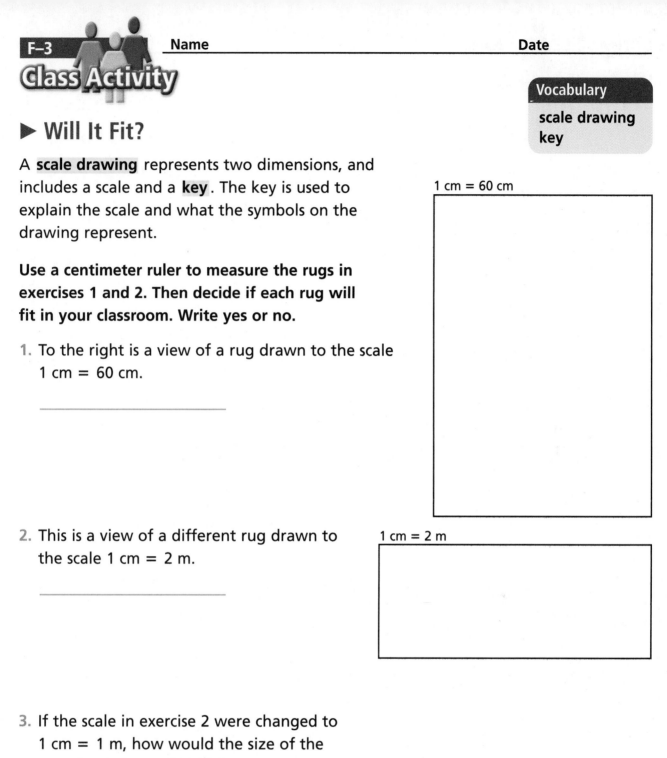

1 cm = 60 cm

1 cm = 2 m

3. If the scale in exercise 2 were changed to 1 cm = 1 m, how would the size of the actual rug change? Explain your answer.

   _____

   _____

   _____

   _____

Name _____ **Date** _____

▶ Draw to Scale

Choose an object in your classroom with a rectangular shape, such as your desktop or a window. Use the quarter-inch grid below to make a scale drawing of the object. Include a key to explain your scale.

Explore Scale Drawings

Vocabulary

floor plan

▶ Discuss a Floor Plan

When interior designers draw a **floor plan** of a room, they often suggest where furniture should be placed. The floor plan below is a scale drawing of a room.

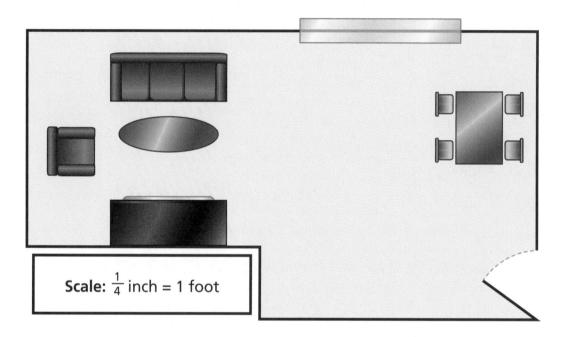

Scale: $\frac{1}{4}$ inch = 1 foot

Use your inch ruler and the scale to answer the questions below.

1. What is the length of the actual sofa? _____

2. What is the length of the actual armchair? _____

3. How much floor space does the actual dining room table take up? _____

4. About how far from the actual sofa is the TV? _____

5. How wide is the actual window? _____

6. Explain why you cannot determine the height of the window.

   _____

7. Draw a bookshelf in the room. What is the width and the depth of the bookshelf you drew? What is its actual width and actual depth?

   _____

   _____

Class Activity

▶ Make a Scale Drawing

The table on the right describes a backyard and its features.

On the grid below, make a scale drawing of the backyard and include all of the features.

• Choose a scale for your drawing and make a key.

• Draw the border of the backyard.

• Choose a location for each feature in the backyard and draw each to scale.

Actual Dimensions

Yard: 400 sq ft
Patio: 10 ft by 12 ft
Picnic table: 4 ft by 6 ft
Children's pool: 4 ft in diameter
Bench: 1 ft by 3 ft

You Choose the Dimensions

Flower garden: _____
Sandbox: _____

Is each pair of figures similar? Circle yes or no.

1.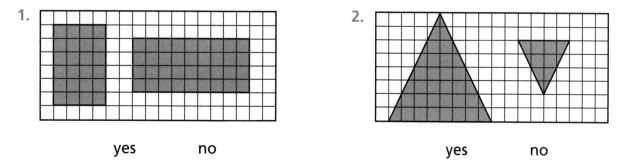

yes   no

2.

yes   no

3. Draw a similar triangle with sides twice as long as the given triangle.

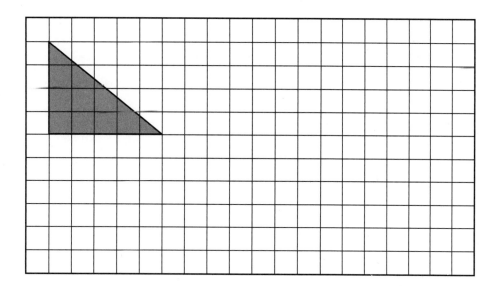

4. Write the missing measurement.

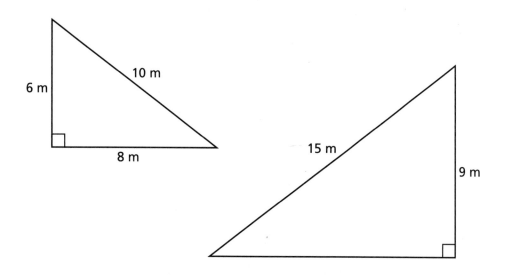

Use the scale to solve for _n_. Show your work.

5. 1 in. = 5 ft
   4 in. = _n_ ft

   _____

6. $\frac{1}{2}$ in. = 1 mi
   $3\frac{1}{2}$ in. = _n_ mi

   _____

7. 1 cm = 3 km
   _n_ cm = 7.5 km

   _____

8. This scale drawing shows that the distance from Orrville to Beetown is 60 km. What is the distance from Orrville to King City?

   _____

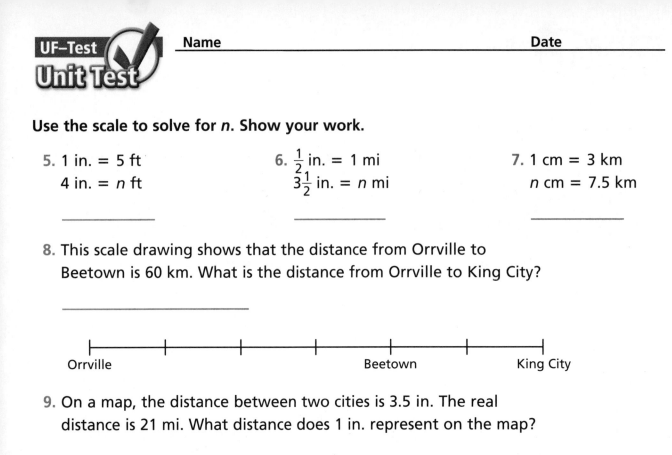

9. On a map, the distance between two cities is 3.5 in. The real distance is 21 mi. What distance does 1 in. represent on the map?

   _____

10. **Extended Response** Make a scale drawing of a rug that measures 9 feet by 12 feet. Include a key.

Glossary

acre A measure of land area. An acre is equal to 4,840 square yards.

acute angle An angle whose measure is less than 90°.

acute triangle A triangle with three acute angles.

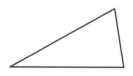

addend One of two or more numbers added together to find a sum.

Example:

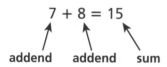

add on Find the difference between two numbers by adding to the smaller number to get the greater number.

angle A figure formed by two rays with a common endpoint.

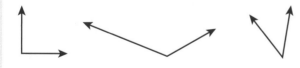

apex The vertex of a cone.

area The amount of surface covered by a figure.

array An arrangement of objects, symbols, or numbers in rows and columns.

Associative Property of Addition Grouping the addends in different ways does not change the sum.

Example: 3 + (5 + 7) = 15
(3 + 5) + 7 = 15

Associative Property of Multiplication Grouping the factors in different ways does not change the product.

Example: 3 × (5 × 7) = 105
(3 × 5) × 7 = 105

axis A line, usually horizontal or vertical, that is labeled with numbers or words to show the meaning of a graph.

bar graph A graph that uses bars to show data.

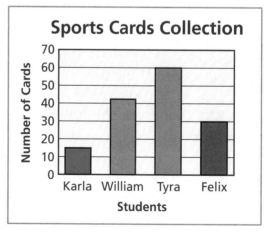

Glossary (Continued)

base For a triangle or parallelogram, a base is any side. For a trapezoid, a base is either of the parallel sides. For a prism, a base is one of the congruent parallel faces. For a pyramid, the base is the face that does not touch the vertex of the pyramid.

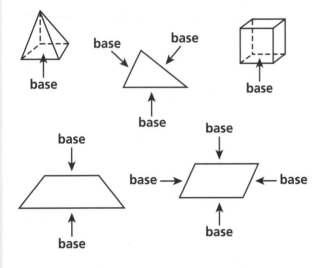

billion One thousand million.

billionth One thousandth of a millionth.

C

capacity A measure of how much a container can hold.

Celsius The metric temperature scale.

centimeter A unit of measure in the metric system that equals one hundredth of a meter. 1 cm = 0.01 m

change minus A change situation that can be represented by subtraction. In a change minus situation, the starting number, the change, or the result will be unknown.

Example:

Unknown Start	Unknown Change	Unknown Result
$n - 2 = 3$	$5 - n = 3$	$5 - 2 = n$

change plus A change situation that can be represented by addition. In a change plus situation, the starting number, the change, or the result will be unknown.

Example:

Unknown Start	Unknown Change	Unknown Result
$n + 2 = 5$	$3 + n = 5$	$3 + 2 = n$

circle A plane figure that forms a closed path so that all the points on the path are the same distance from a point called the center.

circle graph A graph that uses parts of a circle to show data.

Zak's Book Collection

circumference The distance around a circle.

Collection Situations Situations that involve putting together (joining) or taking apart (separating) groups.

column A part of a table or array that contains items arranged vertically.

combination An arrangement of elements.

common denominator A common multiple of two or more denominators.

Example: 6 could be used as a common denominator for $\frac{1}{2}$ and $\frac{1}{3}$.

$$\frac{1}{2} = \frac{3}{6} \quad \frac{1}{3} = \frac{2}{6}$$

Commutative Property of Addition The order of addends does not change the sum.

Example: $3 + 8 = 11$
$8 + 3 = 11$

Commutative Property of Multiplication The order of factors does not change the product.

Example: $3 \times 8 = 24$
$8 \times 3 = 24$

comparison situation Two amounts are compared to find which is more, which is less, and how much more or less.

complementary angles Angles having a sum of 90°.

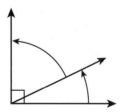

complex figure A figure made by combining simple geometric figures like rectangles and triangles.

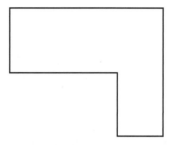

composite number A number greater than 1 that has more than one factor pair. Examples of composite numbers are 4, 15, and 45. The factor pairs of 4 are: 1 and 4, 2 and 2.

cone A solid figure with a curved base and a single vertex.

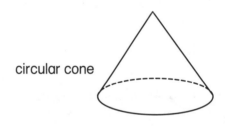

circular cone

congruent Exactly the same size and shape.

Example: Triangles *ABC* and *PQR* are congruent.

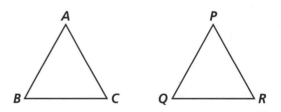

coordinate A number that determines the position of a point in one direction.

counterexample An example that proves that a general statement is false.

Glossary (Continued)

cube A solid figure that has 6 faces that are congruent squares.

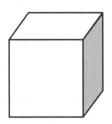

cubic centimeter A metric unit for measuring volume. It is the volume of a cube with one-centimeter edges.

cubic meter A metric unit for measuring volume. It is the volume of a cube with one-meter edges.

cubic unit A unit of volume equal to the volume of a cube with all edges one unit long.

Example: Cubic centimeters and cubic inches are units of volume.

cup A U.S. customary unit of capacity equal to half a pint.

D

data A collection of information.

decimeter A unit of measure in the metric system that equals one tenth of a meter. 1 dm = 0.1 m

degree A unit for measuring angles. Also a unit for measuring temperature. (See Celsius and Fahrenheit.)

denominator The number below the bar in a fraction.

Example: 4 is the denominator.

$\frac{3}{4}$ ◄── denominator

diagonal A line segment connecting two vertices that are not next to each other.

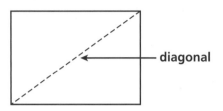

diameter A line segment from one side of a circle to the other through the center. Also the length of that segment.

difference The result of a subtraction.

Example: 54 − 37 = 17

└── difference

digit Any of the symbols 0, 1, 2, 3, 4, 5, 6, 7, 8, or 9.

Digit-by-Digit A method used to solve a division problem.

Example:

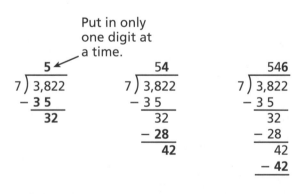

Put in only one digit at a time.

dimension The height, length, or width.

Examples:

A line segment has only length, so it has *one* dimension.

A rectangle has length and width, so it has *two* dimensions.

A cube has length, width, and height, so it has *three* dimensions.

Distributive Property You can multiply a sum by a number, or multiply each addend by the number and add the products; the result is the same.

Example:

$$3 \times (2 + 4) = (3 \times 2) + (3 \times 4)$$
$$3 \times 6 \quad = \quad 6 \quad + \quad 12$$
$$18 \quad = \quad 18$$

Divisible A number is divisible by another number if the quotient is a whole number with no remainder.

Example: 15 is divisible by 5 because $15 \div 5 = 3$

dot array An arrangement of dots in rows and columns.

double bar graph Data is compared by using pairs of bars drawn next to each other.

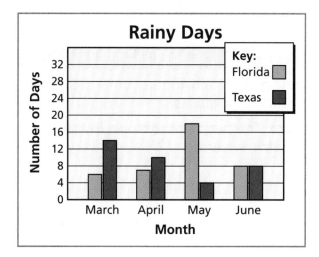

edge A line segment that forms as a side of a two-dimensional figure or the part of a three-dimensional figure where two faces meet.

elapsed time The amount of time that passes from the start of an event to its end.

equal groups Having the same number of objects in more than one group.

equation A statement that two expressions are equal. An equation always has an equals sign.

Example: $32 + 35 = 67$

equilateral Having all equal sides.

Example: An equilateral triangle

equivalent Representing the same number.

equivalent fractions Two or more fractions that represent the same number.

estimate Find about how many or how much. A reasonable guess about a measurement or answer.

even number A whole number that is a multiple of 2. An even number ends with a 0, 2, 4, 6, or 8.

Example: 68 is an even number because it is a multiple of 2; $2 \times 34 = 68$.

Glossary (Continued)

example A specific instance that demonstrates a general statement.

expanded form A way of writing a number that shows the value of each of its digits.

Example: Expanded form of 835:
800 + 30 + 5
8 hundreds + 3 tens + 5 ones

Expanded Notation A strategy used to solve multiplication and division problems.

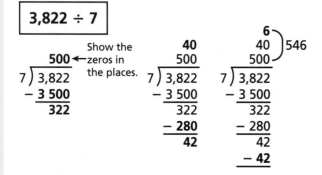

expression A combination of one or more numbers, variables, or numbers and variables with one or more operations.

Examples: 4
6x
6x − 5
7 + 4

face A flat surface of a three-dimensional figure.

factor One of two or more numbers multiplied together to make a product.
Example:

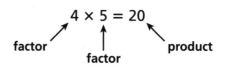

Fahrenheit The temperature scale used in the United States.

floor plan A scale drawing of a room as seen from above.

foot A U.S. customary unit of length equal to 12 inches.

function A consistent relationship between two sets of numbers. Each number in one of the sets is paired with exactly one number in the other set. A function can be shown in a chart, or as a set of ordered pairs.

Example: The relationship between yards and feet.

Yards	1	2	3	4	5	6	7
Feet	3	6	9	12	15	18	21

G

gallon A U.S. customary unit of capacity equal to 4 quarts.

gram The basic unit of mass in the metric system.

greater than (>) A symbol used when comparing two numbers. The greater number is given first.

Example: 33 > 17
33 is greater than 17.

greatest Largest.

H

half turn A 180° rotation.

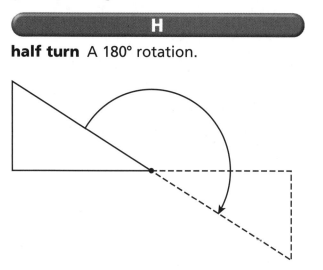

height The perpendicular distance from a base of a figure to the highest point.

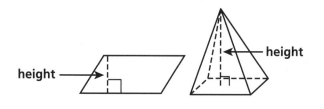

hexagon A six-sided polygon.

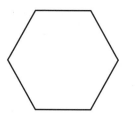

histogram A graph in which bars are used to display how frequently data occurs between intervals.

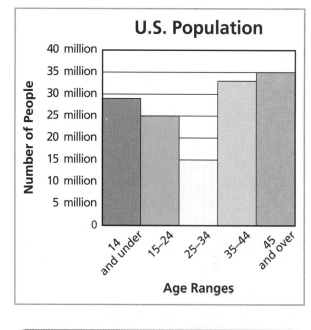

I

Identity Property of Multiplication The product of 1 and any number equals that number.

Example: 10 × 1 = 10

improper fraction A fraction whose numerator is greater than or equal to the denominator.

Example: $\frac{3}{2}$

inch A U.S. customary unit of length.

inequality A statement that two expressions are not equal.

Examples: 2 < 5
4 + 5 > 12 − 8

inverse operations Opposite or reverse operations that undo each other. Addition and subtraction are inverse operations. Multiplication and division are inverse operations.

Examples: 4 + 6 = 10, so 10 − 6 = 4
3 × 9 = 27, so 27 ÷ 9 = 3

Glossary (Continued)

isosceles trapezoid A trapezoid with a pair of opposite congruent sides.

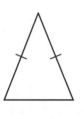

isosceles triangle A triangle with at least two equal sides.

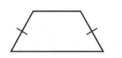

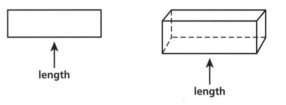

K

key A ratio that shows the real distances represented on a map or a scale drawing.

kilogram A unit of mass in the metric system that equals one thousand grams. 1 kg = 1,000 g

kiloliter A unit of capacity in the metric system that equals one thousand liters. 1 kL = 1,000 L

kilometer A unit of length in the metric system that equals one thousand meters. 1 km = 1,000 m

L

leading A comparing sentence containing language that suggests which operation to use to solve the problem.

Example: What is the *total* of 11 and 17?

least Smallest.

least common denominator The least common multiple of two denominators.
Example: 6 is the least common denominator of $\frac{1}{2}$ and $\frac{1}{3}$.

length The measure of a line segment, or of one side or edge of a figure.

less than (<) A symbol used when comparing two numbers. The smaller number is given first.

Example: 54 < 78
54 is less than 78.

line A straight path that goes on forever in opposite directions.

Example: line *AB*

line graph A graph that uses a broken line to show changes in data.

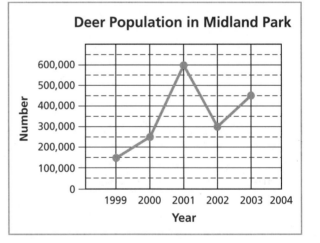

line of symmetry A line that divides a figure into two opposite congruent parts.

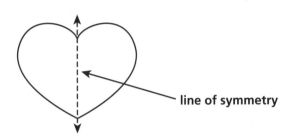

line of symmetry

line segment Part of a line that has two endpoints.

line symmetry A figure has line symmetry if it can be folded along a line to create two halves that match exactly.

Linked Multiplication Column Table A Multiplication Column Table that also has a column showing the unit that links the terms in each ratio.

Example: This table shows the ratios of two rates, $3 per day and $5 per day, and the linking unit, days.

	Noreen	Tim
Days	③	⑤
0	0	0
1	3	5
2	6	10
3	9	15
4	12	20

liter The basic unit of capacity in the metric system.

M

mass The measure of the amount of matter in an object.

mean (average) The sum of the values in a set of data divided by the number of pieces of data in the set.

Example: 75, 84, 89, 91, 101
75 + 84 + 89 + 91 + 101 = 440,
then 440 ÷ 5 = 88. The mean is 88.

measure of central tendency The mean, median, or mode of a set of numbers.

median The middle number in a set of ordered numbers. For an even number of numbers, the median is the average of the two middle numbers.

Examples: 13 26 34 47 52
The median for this set is 34.
8 8 12 14 20 21
The median for this set is
(12 + 14) ÷ 2 = 13.

meter The basic unit of length in the metric system.

milligram A unit of mass in the metric system that equals one thousandth of a gram. 1 mg = 0.001 g

milliliter A unit of capacity in the metric system that equals one thousandth of a liter. 1 mL = 0.001 L

Glossary (Continued)

millimeter A unit of length in the metric system that equals one thousandth of a meter. 1 mm = 0.001 m

misleading A comparing sentence containing language that may trick you into doing the wrong operation.

> **Example:** John's age is 3 *more* than Jessica's. If John is 12, how old is Jessica?

mixed number A number represented by a whole number and a fraction that is less than 1.

> **Example:** $4\frac{2}{3}$

mode The number that appears most frequently in a set of numbers.

> **Example:** 2, 4, 4, 4, 5, 7, 7
> 4 is the mode in this set of numbers.

Multiplication Column Table A table made of two columns from a multiplication table.

Days	Dollars
0	0
1	3
2	6
3	9
4	12
5	15
6	18
7	21
8	24
9	27

multiplication table A table that shows the product of each pair of numbers in the left column and top row.

Multiplication Table Puzzle A two-by-two table that is a part of a multiplication table, with one missing number.

	3	7
2	6	14
4	◯	28

multiplier The factor used to multiply the numerator and denominator to create an equivalent fraction.

> **Example:** A multiplier of 3 changes $\frac{2}{3}$ to $\frac{6}{9}$.

N

negative number A number less than zero.

> **Examples:** −1, −23, and −3.5 are negative numbers.

net A flat pattern that can be folded to make a solid figure.

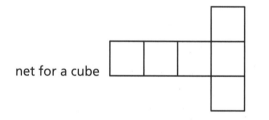

net for a cube

non-unit fraction A fraction with a numerator greater than 1.

> **Examples:** $\frac{3}{4}$ or $\frac{4}{8}$.

number sentence Describes how numbers or expressions are related to each other using one of the symbols =, <, or >. The types of number sentences are equations and inequalities.

> **Examples:** 25 + 25 = 50
> 13 < 8 + 2

numerator The number above the bar in a fraction.

Example: The numerator is 2.

$\frac{2}{3}$ ← numerator

O

oblique lines Lines that are not parallel or perpendicular.

obtuse angle An angle greater than a right angle and less than a straight angle.

obtuse triangle A triangle with one obtuse angle.

odd number A whole number that is not a multiple of 2. An odd number ends with 1, 3, 5, 7, and 9.

Example: 73 is an odd number because it is not a multiple of 2.

one-dimensional Having only length as a measure. A line segment is one-dimensional.

Order of Operations A set of rules that state the order in which operations should be done.
STEPS:
Compute inside parentheses first.
Multiply and divide from left to right.
Add and subtract from left to right.

ordered pair A pair of numbers that shows the position of a point on a graph.

Example: The ordered pair (3, 4) represents a point 3 units to the right of the y-axis and 4 units above the x-axis.

origin The point (0, 0) on a two-dimensional coordinate grid.

ounce A unit of weight or capacity in the U.S. customary system equal to one sixteenth of a pound or one eighth of a cup.

over-estimate An estimate that is greater than the actual amount.

Example: A shirt costs $26.47 and a pair of jeans cost $37.50. You can make an over-estimate by rounding $26.47 to $30 and $37.50 to $40 to be sure you have enough money to pay for the clothes.

P

parallel The same distance apart at every point.

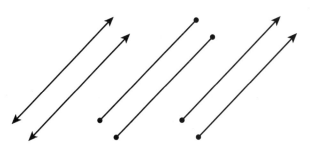

Glossary (Continued)

parallelogram A quadrilateral with both pairs of opposite sides parallel.

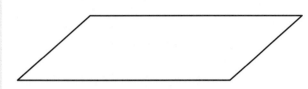

parentheses Symbols used to group numbers together.

7 + (3 × 4) = 19

parentheses

partial products Products of the smaller problems in the Rectangle Sections method of multiplying.

Example: The partial products are highlighted.

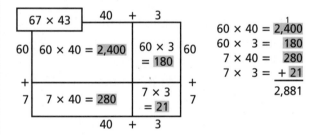

pentagon A polygon with five sides.

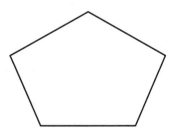

percent A ratio that compares a number to 100. The symbol % means *percent*.

perimeter The distance around a figure.

perpendicular Lines, line segments, or rays are perpendicular if they form right angles.

Example: These two line segments are perpendicular.

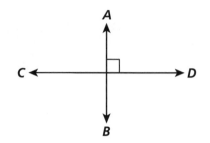

pi A number equal to the circumference of a circle divided by its diameter, or about 3.14. Pi is often represented by the symbol π.

pint A U.S. customary unit of capacity equal to half a quart.

place value The value assigned to the place that a digit occupies in a number.

Example: **235**

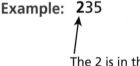

The 2 is in the hundreds place, so its value is 200.

plane A flat surface that extends without end.

polygon A closed plane figure with sides made of straight line segments.

pound A unit of weight in the U.S. customary system.

prime number A number greater than 1 that has 1 and itself as the only factor pair. Examples of prime numbers are 2, 7, and 13. The only factor pair of 7 is 1 and 7.

prism A solid figure with two congruent parallel bases joined by rectangular faces.

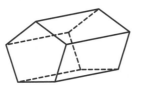

pentagonal prism

probability A number between 0 and 1 that represents the chance of an event happening.

product The result of a multiplication.

Example: $9 \times 7 = 63$

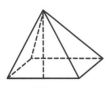

product

proof A demonstration of the truth of a general statement.

proportion An equation that shows two equivalent ratios.

Example: $6 : 10 = 9 : 15$

pyramid A solid with a polygon for a base whose vertices are all joined to a single point.

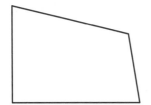

Q

quadrilateral A two-dimensional figure with four sides.

quart A U.S. customary unit of capacity.

quarter turn A 90° rotation.

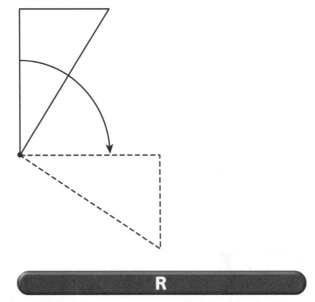

R

radius A line segment that connects the center of a circle to any point on that circle. Also the length of that line segment.

range The difference between the greatest number and the least number in a set.

ratio A comparison of two or more quantities in the same units.

Glossary (Continued)

Ratio Table A table that shows equivalent ratios.

Example: This table show ratios equivalent to the basic ratio, 3 : 5.

③	⑤
0	0
3	5
6	10
9	15
12	20
15	25
18	30
21	35

Rectangle Rows A method used to solve multiplication problems.

Example:

67 × 43	43	
60	$\begin{array}{r} \overset{1}{4}3 \\ \times\ 60 \\ \hline 2,580 \end{array}$	$\begin{array}{r} 2,580 \\ +\ 301 \\ \hline 2,881 \end{array}$
+ 7	$\begin{array}{r} \overset{2}{4}3 \\ \times\ 7 \\ \hline 301 \end{array}$	

Rectangle Sections A method used to solve multiplication and division problems.

Example:

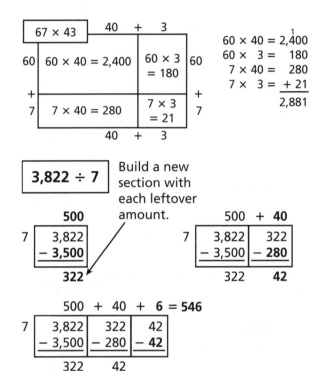

$$67 \times 43$$

	40 + 3	
60	60 × 40 = 2,400	60 × 3 = 180
+ 7	7 × 40 = 280	7 × 3 = 21
	40 + 3	

$$\begin{array}{r} 60 \times 40 = \overset{1}{2,400} \\ 60 \times\ 3 =\quad 180 \\ 7 \times 40 =\quad 280 \\ 7 \times\ 3 = +\ 21 \\ \hline 2,881 \end{array}$$

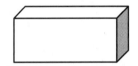

3,822 ÷ 7   Build a new section with each leftover amount.

	500
7	$\begin{array}{r} 3,822 \\ -\ 3,500 \\ \hline 322 \end{array}$

	500	+ 40
7	$\begin{array}{r} 3,822 \\ -\ 3,500 \\ \hline 322 \end{array}$	$\begin{array}{r} 322 \\ -\ 280 \\ \hline 42 \end{array}$

500 + 40 + **6** = **546**

7	$\begin{array}{r} 3,822 \\ -\ 3,500 \\ \hline 322 \end{array}$	$\begin{array}{r} 322 \\ -\ 280 \\ \hline 42 \end{array}$	$\begin{array}{r} 42 \\ -\ 42 \end{array}$

rectangular prism A solid that has congruent rectangular bases.

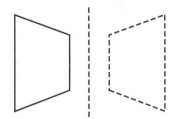

reflection A transformation that flips a figure onto a congruent image. Sometimes called a *flip*.

reflex angle An angle greater than 180°.

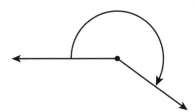

remainder The number left over after dividing a number by a number that does not divide it evenly.

Example: 43 ÷ 5 = 8 R3

The remainder is 3.

Repeated Groups Groups with the same number of objects are Repeated Groups.

Example: 2 + 2 + 2 = 6

There are 3 repeated groups of 2.

rhombus A parallelogram with congruent sides.

right angle An angle that measures 90°.

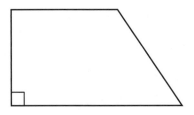

right trapezoid A trapezoid with at least one right angle.

right triangle A triangle with one right angle.

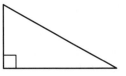

rotation A turn. A transformation that turns a figure so that each point stays an equal distance from a single point, the center of rotation.

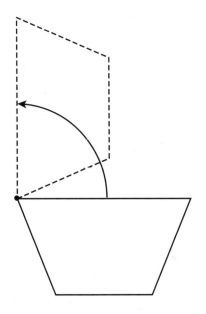

rotational symmetry The property of a figure that allows it to fit exactly on itself in less than one full rotation.

round To find the nearest ten, hundred, thousand, or some other place value.

Example: 463 rounded to the nearest ten is 460.
463 rounded to the nearest hundred is 500.

row A part of a table or array that contains items arranged horizontally.

• • • • •

Glossary (Continued)

S

scale Numbers or marks arranged at regular intervals that are used for measurement or to establish position.

scale drawing A drawing that is made in proportion to the size of a real object.

scalene A triangle with no equal sides is a scalene triangle.

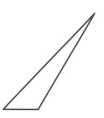

Short cut A method used to solve multiplication problems.

Example: 43 × 67 =

Step 1	Step 2	Step 3	Step 4	Step 5
$\overset{2}{4}3$	$\overset{2}{4}3$	$\overset{2}{4}3$	$\overset{1}{\underset{2}{4}}3$	$\overset{1}{\underset{2}{4}}3$
× 67	× 67	× 67	× 67	× 67
1	301	301	301	301
		0	2,580	2,580
				2,881

similar Having the same shape but not necessarily the same size.

similar figures

simplify To find a result. To rewrite a fraction as an equivalent fraction with a smaller numerator and denominator.

Example: $\frac{3}{6} = \frac{1}{2}$

situation equation An equation that shows the action or the relationship in a problem.

Example: 35 + n = 40

slant height The height of a triangular face of a pyramid.

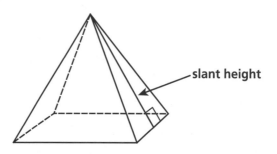

slant height

solution equation An equation that shows the operation to perform in order to solve the problem.

Example: n = 40 − 35

square A rectangle with four congruent sides.

square number The product of a whole number and itself.

Example: 3 × 3 = 9
9 is a square number.

square unit A unit of area equal to the area of a square with one-unit sides.

Examples: square meters and square inches

square yard A unit of area equal to the area of a square with one-yard sides.

standard form The form of a number written using digits.

Example: 2,145

straight angle An angle of 180°.

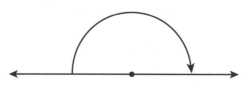

sum The result of an addition.

Example:

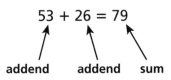

supplementary angles Angles having a sum of 180°.

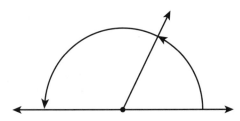

surface area The total area of the two-dimensional surfaces around the outside of a three-dimensional figure.

T

table Data arranged in rows and columns.

three-dimensional Having length measurements in three directions, perpendicular to each other.

ton A unit of weight or mass that equals 2,000 pounds.

tonne A metric unit of mass that equals 1,000 kilograms.

transformation A rule that results in a change of position, orientation, or size of a figure.

translation A transformation that moves a figure along a straight line without turning or flipping. Sometimes called a *slide*.

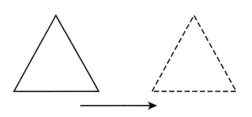

trapezoid A quadrilateral with one pair of parallel sides.

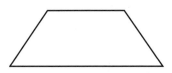

triangle A polygon with three sides.

two-dimensional Having length measurements in two directions, perpendicular to each other.

U

under-estimate An estimate that is less than the actual amount.

Example: A shirt costs $26.47 and a pair of jeans cost $37.50. If you brought $60 to pay for the clothes because you rounded $26.47 to $25 and $37.50 to $35, you made an under-estimate and did not have enough money.

ungroup Rewrite a mixed number with a different whole number and fraction part.

Example: $4\frac{2}{3} = 3\frac{5}{3}$

unit A standard of measurement.

Examples: Centimeters, pounds, inches, and so on.

Glossary (Continued)

unit fraction A fraction with a numerator of 1.
Examples: $\frac{1}{2}$ and $\frac{1}{10}$

unsimplify Rewrite a fraction as an equivalent fraction with a greater numerator and denominator.
Examples: $\frac{1}{2} = \frac{3}{6}$

V

variable A letter or symbol that represents a number in an expression.

vertex A point that is shared by two arms of an angle, two sides of a polygon, or edges of a solid figure. The point of a cone.

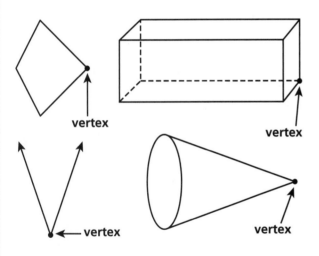

vertex · vertex · vertex · vertex

view A two-dimensional figure that shows what a solid looks like from the front, side, or top.

volume The measure of the amount of space occupied by an object.

W

width The measure of one side or edge of a figure.

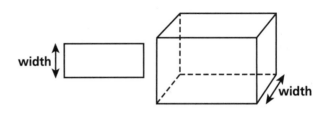

width · width

word form The form of a number written using words instead of digits.
Example: Six hundred thirty-nine

X

x-axis The horizontal axis of a two-dimensional coordinate grid.

x-coordinate A number that represents a point's horizontal distance from the *y*-axis in two dimensions.

Y

y-axis The vertical axis of a two-dimensional coordinate grid.

yard A U.S. customary unit of length equal to 3 feet.

y-coordinate A number that represents a point's vertical distance from the *x*-axis in two dimensions.